Fifty Nature Walks in Southern Illinois

Fifty Nature Walks in Southern Illinois

by Alan McPherson

Cache
River
Press

Vienna, IL
Clearwater, FL

Library of Congress Catalogue Card Number 92-074735
ISBN 0-9627422-3-6

1st edition

Author:
Alan McPherson

Sponsor:
The Southern Illinoisan Newspaper

Publisher:
Cache River Press
Rt. 3, Box 239C
Vienna, IL 62595

Printed in the USA

Cover photo of Observation Overlook Trail by Ned Trovillion.
Back cover photograph courtesy of Les Winkeler/The Southern Illinoisan

Dedicated to

Besse Mae McPherson,

who grew up in southern Illinois and loved the land.

Hill blue among the leaves in summer,
Hill blue among the branches in winter–
Light sea blue at the sand beaches in winter,
Deep sea blue in the deep deep waters
Prairie blue, mountain blue–
Who can pick a pocketful of these blues, a handkerchief of these blues
And go walking, talking, walking as though God gave them a lot of loose change
For spending money, to throw at the birds,
To flip into the tin cups of blind men?

Cheap Blue by Carl Sandburg

Table of Contents

Page Key   Page Number

F   Foreword by Don Pierce for the SIERRA CLUB .... *viii-x*

P   Preface .... **xi-xii**

In   Discovering Southern Illinois **2-11**

SI   Regional Map **12-13**

K   Map with Nature Walks Pinpointed **14-15**

Elizabethtown District

1.   Saline Springs National Historic Site *18-21*
2.   Saline County Conservation Area *22-25*
3.   Stone Face Recreation Site *26-29*
4.   Rim Rock & Pounds Hollow Complex *30-35*
5.   High Knob Recreation Area *36-39*
6.   Garden of the Gods Recreation & Wilderness Area *40-45*
7.   Gibbons Creek Barrens.. *46-49*
8.   Beaver Trail *50-55*
9.   River-to-River Trail *56-61*
10.   Illinois Iron Furnace Recreation Site *62-65*
11.   Tower Rock Recreation Area *66-69*
12.   Cave in Rock State Park *70-75*

Vienna District

13.   Lusk Creek Canyon Nature Preserve............................... *78-83*
14.   Bell Smith Springs Recreation Area................................ *84-91*
15.   Jackson Hollow *92-97*
16.   Millstone Bluff Archeological Site *98-101*
17.   Lake Glendale Recreation Area *102-105*
18.   Dixon Springs State Park *106-109*
19.   Wildcat Bluff & Little Black Slough *110-115*
20.   Heron Pond *116-121*
21.   Section 8 Woods Nature Preserve *122-125*
22.   Limekiln Springs Trail.. *126-129*
23.   Mermet Lake Conservation Area *130-133*
24.   Fort Massac State Park *134-139*
25.   Lake of Egypt Recreation Area.................................... *140-143*
26.   Dutchman Lake *144-147*
27.   Ferne Clyffe State Park... *148-155*

Murphysboro District

28. Crab Orchard National Wildlife Refuge *158-165*
29. Carbondale Nature Places *166-173*
30. Touch of Nature Environmental Center *174-179*
31. Giant City State Park *180-185*
32. Lake Murphysboro State Park *186-189*
33. Kinkaid Lake Trail *190-193*
34. Cedar Lake Trail & Little Cedar Lake Trail *194-199*
35. Pomona Natural Bridge Recreation Area *200-203*
36. Little Grand Canyon Recreation Site *204-207*
37. Oakwood Bottoms, Turkey Bayou & Fountain Bluff *208-213*
38. Devil's Backbone Park *214-217*

Jonesboro District

39. Observation Overlook Trails *220-225*
40. Godwin Trail *226-229*
41. White Pine Trail *230-233*
42. Iron Mountain Trail *234-237*
43. Trail of Tears State Forest *238-243*
44. Lincoln Memorial Site *244-247*
45. Hamburg Hill Trail *248-251*
46. Union County Conservation Area *252-255*
47. North Ripple Hollow & Pine Knob Trail *256-259*
48. Horse Creek Trail *260-263*
49. Sammons Creek Trail *264-267*
50. Horseshoe Lake Conservation Area *268-273*

A-I Additional Southern Illinois Nature Places **274-286**
A-II Helpful Books **288-291**
A-III Animals of Southern Illinois **292-296**
ID Index **297-299**

*R*ub a sensitive finger across one of those globes with bumps where the mountain ranges are located and you can feel a small rise about half way up the Mississippi River. You have found the "Interior Highlands."

*H*ere the hills are forested with oaks, hickories, and some pine. Abundant water flows in numerous streams, sometimes over the rocky surface and sometimes lost to the Swiss-cheese geology below. The water that can remain on the surface converges into the greatest confluence of rivers in North America. In the flood-plains of these rivers are remnants of the once pervasive swamps.

*I*n addition to these dominant natural features, the Interior Highlands also have a distinctive cultural unity.

*M*any of the people who lived away from the more cosmopolitan centers such as St. Louis or Louisville are descendants from "Old-stock" Americans. They migrated into the southern midwest, following Daniel Boone westward from the southern colonies. Most are "Celtic," meaning that they are of Scottish, Welsh or Irish descent. They settled amongst the hills and hollows away from the often flood-ravaged Ohio, Mississippi and Arkansas Rivers.

*T*hese are big rivers. The Great Lakes are to the north, the Great Plains are to the West; but dividing and unifying the Interior Highlands are the Great Rivers.

*W*est of the Mississippi in southern Missouri and northern Arkansas are the Ozarks–a concentric series of broad, flat-topped plateaus surrounding a mountain range far older and craggier than the upstart Rockies and Appalachians.

F

*S*outh of the Arkansas River in central Arkansas are the Oachitas–an array of relatively narrow-ridged Mountains, arranged like teeth on a saw.

*E*ast of the Mississippi are the Interior Low Plateaus. These are the hills of middle to western Kentucky and Tennessee, southwest Ohio, and southern Indiana.

*A*nother one of these plateaus is in southern Illinois. It stretches from Horseshoe Bluff on the Mississippi River near Grand Tower to Battery Rock near Cave in Rock on the Ohio. Actually, this plateau is a "cuesta." *Whatsa "Cuesta"?*

*A*n excellent example is the Shawnee Hills area. This region spans the foot of Illinois like an ankle strap. Looking down on the band you see an asymmetrical plateau broken by the erosive action of numerous streams, including Grand Pierre, Lusk and Bay.

*I*n character with any good "cuesta" (pronounced "kwesta" or "Kwaysta") one ridge of the plateau has a shallow grade (in the case of the Shawnee Hills this is the north slope) and the opposite ridge has a steeper grade (like the south slope of the Shawnee Hills toward the Ohio River flood plain).

*T*he southern edge of the Shawnee Hills offers some of the best "views" in Illinois. The scenic drama of this portion of the "cuesta" is accentuated by the contrasting landscape at the toe of Illinois. Not really a part of the Interior Highlands topographically, the southern-most tip of Illinois is essentially the northernmost tip of the Gulf Coast Plain. This region is highly affected by big rivers of the Midwest. The topography is flat. Instead of upland forests, rows of crops prevail, but not everywhere.

*I*n the Cache River watershed between the central portion of the Shawnee Hills and Ohio River, swamps reminiscent of the deep

F

south create an altogether different experience for those on nature outings. Here the forest floor is a shallow lake, and the trees are cypress and tupelo gum.

*T*he Cache is a wonderful place to visit, a rare treat for those in the know. Good trail information about the Cache and Interior Highlands areas is sparse, but the demand is considerable.

*T*o help satisfy this demand, members of the Upland Group of the Indiana Chapter of the Sierra Club had the idea to develop a guide to nature walks for their interior low plateau. These Hoosiers are to be commended for encouraging Alan McPherson to write **NATURE WALKS IN SOUTHERN INDIANA**.

*F*ortunately, McPherson also has spent considerable time in the Shawnee/Cache region.

*T*ake advantage of McPherson's delightful introduction to deep southern Illinois. Once introduced, walk through the 50 natural areas described in **NATURE WALKS OF SOUTHERN ILLINOIS.** Try to gain the kind of familiarity needed to inspire true devotion. Once devoted, contact the Sierra Club or other conservation organizations. These groups can tell you more about other places to visit; they can also let you know what needs to be done to protect and restore the place you have learned to love.

Don Pierce,
for the Illinois Chapter of the Sierra Club

F

*S*outhern Illinois residents and visitors are fortunate in having an abundance of natural beauty to enjoy. The moderate climate permits year round outdoor activities in a diverse and unique North American landscape. The following compilation of nature walks describes 50 and more outdoor areas that may be explored on foot.

Lake Scene

*T*here are trails for all seasons: trails that lead to deep cool and refreshing forested ravines and coves, trails in populated urban and suburban parklands, trails along ridgetops with open panoramic year round vistas, trails leading through renewing spring wildflower meadows and up slopes ablaze in autumn's deciduous colors and trails that lead out to mysterious wetlands on boardwalks.

*W*ith *Fifty Nature Walks in Southern Illinois,* the walking enthusiast will be able to locate over 100 trails ranging from short and easy to long and rugged. The majority of the nature walks can be completed in one day. The first four sections of the guidebook include trails located in the 12 counties south of S.R. Illinois 13 and between the Mississippi and Ohio Rivers. The material was gathered and the trails photographed between 1986 and 1992. All write-ups have been checked for accuracy by the administering authorities.

*M*aps, line drawings and black and white photographs accompany the writeups. A capsule heading at the top of the page lists location, U.S.G.S. Map, trail distance, acreage, activities and fees, when applicable. The main focus of each write-up is its outstanding features, trailhead locations, trail surface, and a guide to highway travel direction.

*M*ore than a trail guide, the guidebook explores fauna, flora, folklore, history, geology, recreational sites and activities to further enhance your experience.

Alan McPherson

P

A special thanks with deep gratitude to all individuals who generously contributed to the making of this book. The Author and Publisher are grateful for the help of the Forest Service personnel of southern Illinois. They also thank Randy Tindall of Enterprise South for photographic work, Rick Goldstein and Joe Oberuc for editing, Carolina Jiménez for design work, and especially Rick Linton, of Imagery, for map composition. Finally, most of all, we thank the numerous individuals who encouraged us to describe the natural wealth and beauty of southern Illinois.

Southern Illinois's natural beauty and mild climate are ideal to explore on foot year around. Spring, fall, and even winter are ideal seasons to go for a hike in the "Shawnee Hills." Good hiking can occur during summer but temperatures and humidity are high and can last for several weeks, especially in July and August. Despite the ongoing environmental alteration and destruction by urbanization and agricultural development, anyone in the south central eastern United States will discover within a day's drive prairie-like barrens or glades, creeks, caves, waterfalls, cliffs, forests, swamps and other wetlands in "Little Egypt," the "Land Between the Rivers."

Nature walks are plentiful in southern Illinois especially in the 265,135 acre Shawnee National Forest that is headquartered in Harrisburg, Illinois with ranger district offices in Elizabethtown, Vienna, Murphysboro and Jonesboro. To fully appreciate the special spirit of each place you must head out on foot. Individuals within private organizations and separate levels of government have helped to establish a remarkable variety of institutions and parklands in the southern Illinois "Ozarks." The main mission of this trail book is to guide lovers of the outdoors to 50 and more natural areas that are publicly accessible in southern Illinois. In this book, southern Illinois is defined as the land area roughly south of S.R. 13 to the Mississippi and Ohio River boundaries with Missouri and Kentucky. The experiences described in the book range from state to city park trails and nature preserves to wilderness backpacking. The majority of the experiences are found in Shawnee National Forest lands.

*F*or references the nature walks are divided and listed by the four national forest administrative units or regional districts: Elizabethtown, Vienna, Murphysboro and Jonesboro. The walks are numbered and correspond to a regional map at the beginning of each of the four sections. The majority of the trails can be completed in one day or less. The trails in each section or district are listed East to West and then North to South. To ensure accuracy, all of the following nature walks were checked by the administering authorities. Each write-up includes capsule information, headings of location, topographical maps, trail distance, acreage, activities and fees when appropriate. The main focus of each hike includes a trail description, what to expect and how to arrive at the trailhead. Black and white photographs, trail and road maps accompany each chapter. Take along this book on your walks and record your findings and experiences!

*O*rganizing the book according to natural divisions was considered but proved to be difficult. The natural divisions in southern Illinois include: the Greater and Lesser Shawnee Hills, the Lower Mississippi River Bottomlands south section, the Ozark Division south section and the Coastal Plain Division which includes the Cretaceous Hill section and the Bottomland section.

*N*o special skills are required to be a walker but to further enhance your enjoyment and safety in the outdoors there are tips that are worthy of mention. Plan and study ahead your special needs for either a short walk, day hike or several backpack overnights. Consider your physical comfort and limitations in our humid continental climate. Soft-soled footwear such as quality tennis shoes or lightweight hiking shoes are best for the terrain of southern Illinois. The average walking speed is two to three mph or 20 minutes per mile. Of course the rougher and more rugged the trail the more required time to complete the hike. Good fitting and roomy clothing are essential; cotton for summer and wool for winter. Layering, dark clothing, natural wool and some cotton and high-tech synthetics are best for winter. Be cautious of frostbite, hypothermia, and dehydration in winter and heat exhaustion and stroke in summer. Several sporting and outdoor stores have all hiking and backpacking needs in our area.

*S*uggested day pack essentials and/or options may include rainwear (There is 43" annual rainfall.), maps, compass, flashlight, pocket knife, water, butane lighter, first aid kit, whistle, dry food such as fruits and nuts, toilet paper, bug repellent and guidebook to your favorite nature study like birds or geology. A hat, sunglasses, binoculars and the gear should fit nicely in one or two day packs.

*B*ackpacking with overnights will naturally require additional gear, especially in winter. An extra change of clothing and evening wear may include a sweater or light coat, wool socks and a parka. Sleeping gear such as a bag, ground-pad and/or cloth and tent add to the pounds carried. Cooking gear and food will also add to your load and will require heavier shoes for support. Plenty of firewood is available in back country areas, but use only dead or downed wood and take care with fire. Established campgrounds are plentiful throughout southern Illinois. Camping is permitted unless posted in the Shawnee National Forest.

*O*ther overnight items that may be included are candles, repair kits, toilet articles, towel, garden trowel and plastic bags that may serve as emergency raincoats for backpacks or for hikers.

*I*f matches are preferred, you may waterproof the heads with nail polish or other coating material. Generally speaking, gear should

In

be compact, simple and light and in general you can explore without expensive gear. Before leaving always tell your family or friends your hiking plans and make sure your vehicle is road-worthy to take you and others to a set destination and return.

*T*rail quality and their conditions will vary from experience to experience. Few trails are paved and handicapped accessible. Off road vehicles, especially ATV's and heavy horse traffic degrade the trails for hikers. Trail brochures are available at some trailheads such as nature preserves, but some trails are not marked or signed. Trail signing could be improved and the forest service is in the process of doing so but vandalism takes its toll. Possibly in the future, quality trail maintenance could be achieved by an "Adopt-a-Trail" program for families, groups and individuals.

*T*here are seven Congressionally designated wilderness areas in the Shawnee National Forest. These areas have few designated and marked trails but this is changing. These are: Bald Knob (5,918 acres), Bay Creek (2,866 acres), Burden Falls (3,723 acres), Clear Springs (4,730 acres), Garden of the Gods (3,293 acres), Lusk Creek (4,796 acres) and Panther Den (940 acres).

*W*hen planning a hike consider the length of daylight especially during the short days of late fall and winter. Steep hills will cut your hiking time in half. Trail rules may vary but basically all expect fire control, trash and sanitary containment and respect for private property and people. Hikers should be aware of the potential dangers of hunters during the hunting seasons. Accidents have happened. Horsemen and ORV's usage of trails keep overgrown paths cleared but the heavy impact may result in unwanted erosion and rough hiking. Many trails are overgrown at certain times of the year and trail maintenance is not as good as it should be. Off trail exploration is more secure if compass and maps are available. Topographic quadrangle maps, available from the United States Geological Survey, the Shawnee National Forest Service headquarters and regional offices and local outdoor recreation stores feature natural detail with colorful artistic symbols. The topographical maps are of a scale of 1:24,000 or one inch on the map equals 2,000 feet in a real setting. The colors used are somewhat real to life: green for woodland, brown lines for contour earth, blue for water and black for human works. Topographical or "Topo" and other maps may be purchased from:

> Illinois State Geological Survey
> 615 East Peabody Drive
> Champaign, Illinois 61820
> Phone: 217-333-4747

> USDA-Forest Service
> Shawnee National Forest
> 901 S. Commercial Street
> Harrisburg, Illinois 62946

*A*n index providing map locations, local dealers, special items, ordering and price information is available from:

> Chief Mid-Continent Mapping Center
> U.S. Geological Survey
> 1400 Independence
> Rolla, Missouri 65401

*S*everal backpacking and outdoor stores in the larger communities carry topographical maps. Prices vary but expect to pay between $2.25 and $4.00. Consider checking out the Geology section in Morris Library at Southern Illinois University or libraries at other educational institutions and govenment agencies.

*I*nsect pests are also part of being outdoors and southern Illinois has its share of noxious-to-people critters. Chiggers, otherwise known as harvest mites or red bugs are prolific from early spring to late fall. Only the near-invisible larva of this mite (Arachnid) feeds on humans and other animals by dropping off brushy or herbaceous vegetation and piercing the skin. They cause a red welt by injecting a fluid that breaks down the tissue and a tube is formed in which the chigger lives and feeds on blood. The larva bites ankles, waist, arm pits and other protected body areas. Severe itching follows the larva bites. Little can be done after being bitten except to apply itch relief ointments, witch-hazel or take a saltwater bath. Best prevention entails staying away from overgrown meadow-like areas and walking in the middle of paths, applying sulphur dust or ointment around the legs and ankles before entering herbaceous areas. Kerosene is reputed to be ideal but smelly. Drugstore insecticides are also available.

*A*dult North American wood ticks or "dog ticks" are a particular problem in early spring to mid-spring but are also found during warm weather in grassy open areas and woodlands. Never high in numbers, dog ticks are crab-shaped and the largest of the mites, closely related to chiggers. They transmit disease such as Lyme disease and Rocky Mountain Spotted Fever. Ticks feed on the blood by injecting their parasitic mouth parts into the skin.

*T*he Lone Star tick of the south central United States is also found in certain pockets of national forest lands. "Seed" ticks are the

In

newly hatched young larvae of Lone Star ticks and may occur in greater numbers. The small and extremely difficult to see minute "seed" tick is common in grassy areas from June to frost and seed tick bites are similar in appearance to chigger bites. To prevent bites use sulphur, kerosene or commercial spray. Wear long pants, tuck pant legs into boots or socks and tuck shirt into pants. If a tick does attach, use alcohol or petroleum to remove it. Do not leave the infectious head behind.

*T*he female mosquito is a problem in a few areas of southern Illinois. The pesky flying insect is usually common in low swampy areas or poorly drained bottomlands, particularly at sunset, evening and sunrise. The *Culex* species carries diseases such as malaria, but these are rarely transmitted in the United States today. Cutters to citronella, synthetic to organic, there are numerous insect repellents and most hikers have their favorites. Mosquitoes are seldom seen in southern Illinois after mid-September.

*T*he female deer fly, like the female mosquito, needs blood for protein to produce young. Deer flies breed in wet areas and are especially noticeable along lake reservoirs, swamp or wet woodland. A hat, long sleeve shirt and pants help keep them from biting as do certain insecticides or herbal oils. They are strong fliers and will pursue their victims for miles. The insect is usually not noticed after the August 1 but they may persist. The wood eye gnat can be a pest of the eye, ear, nose and mouth in late summer until frost. They attempt to fly into the secretions to lay their eggs. The annoying winged insect seems to follow right along with your hiking steps. Repellents work to a degree.

*O*verall, spiders, or arachnids, are beneficial but there are ones to avoid. Black widows are rarely found in southern Illinois in trash dumps, outhouses, stumps, stonewalls, and beneath objects. They are shy but deadly poisonous, especially to small children however there is an anti-venom. The brown recluse is occasionally found in southern Illinois. An annoying but harmless spider of late summer and early fall is the spiny Wood's Spider or *Micrathera* species that builds webs seemingly everywhere along the trails. Yellow jackets, bees, hornets, and wasps may sting, sometimes repeatedly. Centipedes rarely bite and are non-poisonous. Moistened baking soda is reputed to relieve the sting of insects. Fortunately no fire ants or killer bees are as of yet in the area.

*T*here are many types of snakes found in the area. The common harmless snakes include the garter, water, brown, kirtland, hognose, racers, rat and king. Be advised that non-poisonous snakes will bite if disturbed. Snakes are usually active from April to October and most are basically nocturnal but will venture out in the day. Occasionally hikers will nearly step on a garter or black racer basking in a sunny opening along a trail.

*T*hree species of poisonous snakes are native to southern Illinois. The copperhead and the timber rattlesnake are the only two poisonous snakes found primarily in the undisturbed uplands in southern Illinois. The poisonous water moccasin or cottonmouth, often confused with a harmless water snake, is a swamp reptile that feeds on fish and frogs. The cottonmouth is black, thick-bodied and aquatic. When threatened they open their mouth to expose the white or "cotton" interior that serves as a visual warning. They have a more serious bite than a copperhead, the most common poisonous snake in the area, and are the most life threatening.

*T*he copperhead inhabits high, rocky, dry upland ridges in the southern half of Illinois; however, it is also found under rocks

In

near streams and wood piles. Its bite is rarely fatal. It is difficult to see on the forest floor since the snake's chestnut brown body and red-bronze copper head blends well with the leaf litter. As the rattlesnake, the copperhead and the cottonmouth are pit vipers with retractable hollow fangs and bear live young in late summer. Watch out for this "highland moccasin" when stepping over logs or climbing rock formations since there is no warning of their presence and they will strike at any position.

*T*he timber rattlesnake inhabits similar rocky, hilly terrain as the copperhead. They do not always "rattle" before striking and may lie quietly, hoping to remain unnoticed. The thick body is yellow with black "V"-shaped bands and a dark tail. The rattlesnake bite may be fatal in a few hours if the poison is not extracted or anti-venom injected. Seek help if stricken and try to remain calm as possible to slow down the blood circulation. Snakebite victims in remote areas that are at least two hours away from the nearest medical facility may apply the linear incision and suction method and a broad loose tourniquet with light pressure. However since medical facilities are quickly available, it is probably best to avoid any first aid measures in the field. More people are killed each year by bee stings and lightning strikes than poisonous snakes.

*P*lants like poison ivy (three forms) should be identified and avoided. The noxious plant is fairly common along the trails and if you encounter the vine use rubbing alcohol to remove the oils and then bathe as soon as possible. Poison oak only grows in swampy areas in southern Illinois. Woodland stinging nettle can be painful as can be greenbriar and briars from roses, rasp, black and dewberry canes. The honey locust and hawthorns have very sharp thorns. Japanese honeysuckle can entangle hiking feet. It is

In

remotely possible that an encounter with a skunk may result in being sprayed. Even more remote is a bite from a rabid raccoon or wild dogs. The safety rule for lightning is to seek out dense woods, ravines, ditches and groves of immature trees and not shelter underneath large solitary trees, hilltops, high ground, or rock ledge outcrops. Also remember that spring is tornado season.

*L*earning to identify the variety of flora and fauna of the region will add greatly to the pleasure of your walks.

*C*ampgrounds found throughout southern Illinois are administered by various levels of government and private commercial enterprise.

*A*fter a long hike, treat your feet to a warm soaking, cool rinse, easy drying and maybe some foot powder. Put on a fresh pair of socks if handy. Be flexible and prepared for all your trips in the outdoors. Hike solo or, better yet, with a friend.

*T*rail routes are always changing and new trails are being added, such as in the wilderness areas or the rails-to-trails route from Belknap to Harrisburg, Illinois. The forest service plans to triple the mileage of trails in the Shawnee National Forest over the next decade or less. Old trails are neglected or re-routed, improved or abandoned. Fee rates are always changing and new fees are being added. At this time, the Illinois State park system is considering entrance fees. The Author and Publisher are not responsible for any accidents that may incur while using this guide.

*E*njoy exploring Southern Illinois, its many moods and wonders in your moments of renewal and discovery.

In

Southern Illinois

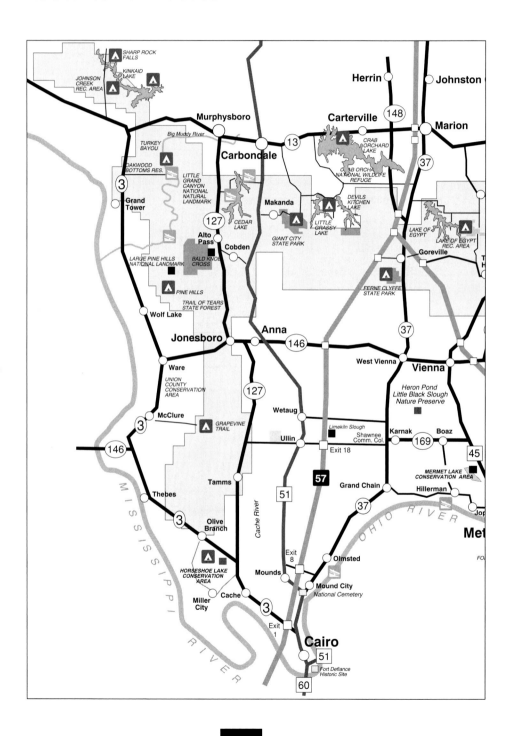

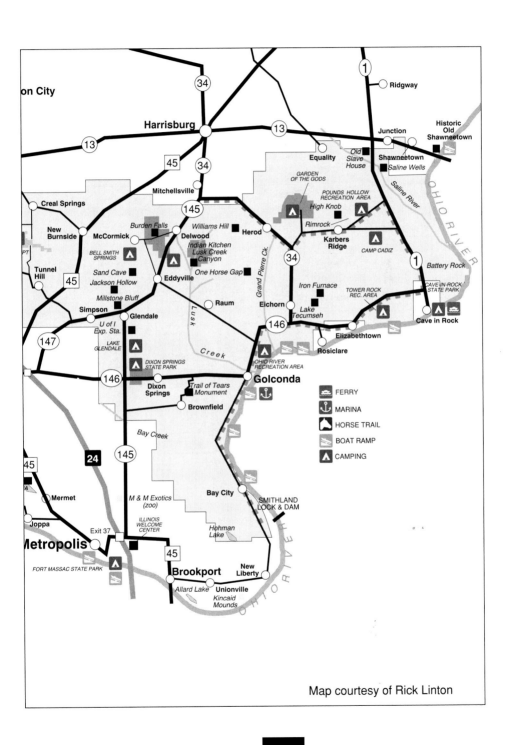

Map courtesy of Rick Linton

SI

Number Key to Sites

• • •

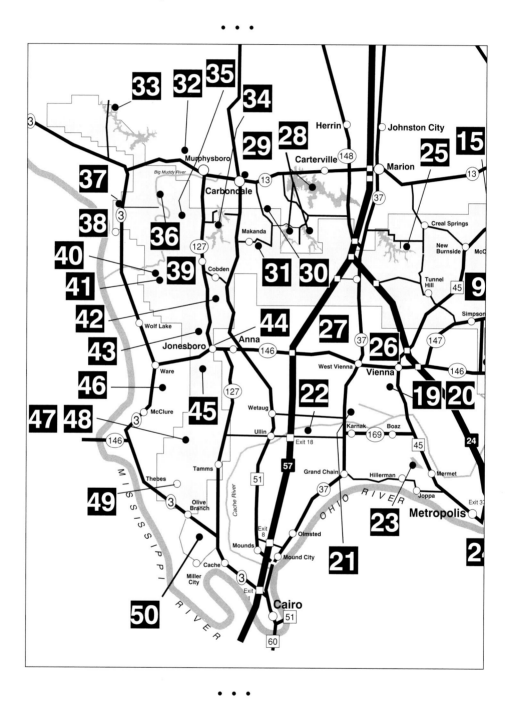

• • •

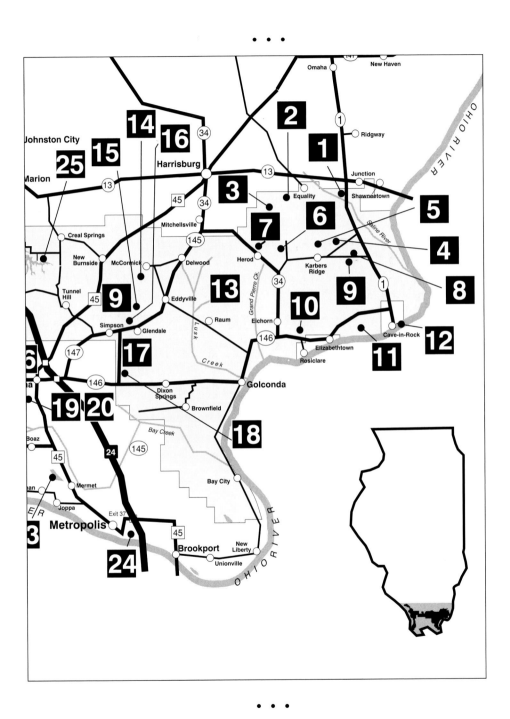

Abbreviations Used:

ATV .... all terrain vehicle
ORV .... off-road vehicle

CCC .... Civilian Conservation Corps

C.R. .... County Road
F.H. .... Forest (service) Highway
F.R. .... Forest (service) Road
I .... Interstate Highway
IL (followed by number) .... Illinois Highway
S.R. .... State Road
U.S. (followed by number) .... United States Highway
U.S.G.S. .... United States Government Survey

IL .... Illinois
KY .... Kentucky
MO .... Missouri

Elizabethtown District

Saline Springs National Historic Site

Old Slave House near Saline Springs

*G*allatin County had two salt springs that produced brine for one of the first salt works companies west of the Alleghenies. One of the springs is located southwest of Equality and the other is at Saline Springs National Historic Site. The Mississippian Indians made salt here as early as the 10th century and as late as the 16th century. In 1803, the Kaskaskia Indians ceded the "Great Salt Spring" to the United States by treaty. Congress refused to sell the salt lands to the public but it did authorize the Secretary of the Treasury to lease the lands to individuals for a royalty. The leases required the holder to produce a certain quantity of salt each year or pay a penalty.

*A*lthough the Northwest Ordinance prohibited slavery in the area, special Territorial laws and Constitutional provisions permitted exceptions for the salines. The leasees abducted slaves or acquired indentured servants and used them extensively in manufacturing salt. The 1820 census for Gallatin County listed 239 slaves.

*I*n 1818 the new State of Illinois received the salines from the U. S. Congress and at first forbade the sale of the land. The commercial production of salt continued until about 1873 when the low price for salt made the expense of extracting it from brine prohibitive. The last operator of Old Spring, as it became known, was John Hart Crenshaw, who built the still standing Slave House two miles north of there.

*T*he Old Salt Spring is easily accessible by car and foot from a gravel road that runs next to the Saline River, southeast of Equality. The short path to the spring is obvious and the site is squared off by timbers and signed. The white crystal brine is still collected by the adventuresome and boiled down to produce a fine grade of salt.

*I*f you enjoy walking more, follow the spring creek one quarter mile north as it winds through the woods to join Saline Creek. Several miles further downstream where Eagle Creek joins the Saline River, the water occasionally turns a whitish color from the concentration of salt.

*T*o reach Saline Springs National Historic Site from I-57 at Marion, Illinois exit #54A-B. Go east onto U. S. 13 and drive about 40 miles to the junction with S.R. 1. Turn south on S.R. 1 and drive three miles, just beyond the Saline River bridge about 0.3 miles turn right/west onto F.R. 1658. Bear right, northwest along the river road about 0.8 miles to the salt spring. You will first pass the canoe or boat launch access near the bridge from where two day trips may be launched to Cave in Rock State Park on the Ohio River. The spring lies just north of the small road dip between two old river-accessible, forest lanes that may also be explored. Saline Springs has been listed on the National Register of Historic Sites since 1973.

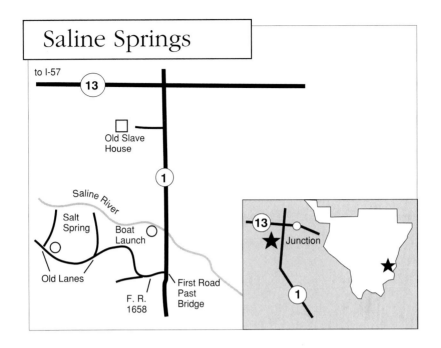

Saline Springs

to I-57

Old Slave House

Saline River

Salt Spring

Boat Launch

Old Lanes

F. R. 1658

First Road Past Bridge

Junction

Saline Springs National Historic Site

• • •

Location:
Equality IL/Gallatin County

U.S.G.S. Map(s):
1:24,000 Equality, Shawneetown

Trail(s) Distance:
30 yards from road to springs, forest service lanes nearby

Activities:
nature walk, nature study, historic site, salt brine collection, canoe boat launch

Fee(s):
none

• • •

1

Saline County Conservation Area

Hikers

*C*omposed of hills, ravines, cliffs, caves, bottomlands and scenic Glen O. Jones Lake, this state of Illinois Conservation property offers the hiker three foot trails that explore the rugged terrain: Wildlife Nature Trail, three-fourths miles, Lake Trail three miles, and Cave Hill Trail three miles. All three trails are well maintained and signed so be prepared for a hiking challenge.

*T*he Wildlife Nature Trail is a brief hillside loop surrounded on four sides by park development. The short woodland path begins and ends near the concession stand and boat dock which are near the park road across from the lake. The self guiding interpretive trail provides great sunset views over the lake when the leaves fall and makes a fine hike with children.

*T*he Lake Trail encircles Glen O. Jones Lake beginning and ending at the concession stand and boat docks. The 105 acre man-made lake was named after a prominent Saline County citizen who served as a state senator. The three mile trail is wooded and follows the high ground around the scenic lake. The path is generally clear but directionally confusing near the inlet due to ATV use so keep in mind where the lake is located. The shoreline is 2.7 miles. This is a good summer-time walk.

*T*he Cave Hill Trail begins near the northwest picnic and playground area next to the main park road loop. The trailhead is marked and there is ample parking available for seven vehicles. The first quarter mile is on state property and the additional 2.75 miles is Shawnee National Forest land. The vehicle wide path has seen ATV use and the clay surface path is very slick when wet. The trail gradually ascends the ridge. Follow the forest path always bearing to the left. Equality Cave near Cave Hill is located about 1.8 miles from the parking area along the east facing hillside about 100 yards from the main trail to Cave Hill.

Even though the entrance is small it has many interconnecting passages formed from centuries of water slowly dissolving the bedrock. The cave is popular with spelunkers. It is easy to go on past the summit of Cave Hill so it is advised to carry a topographical map depicting the summit. Hikers have been known to continue their hike many miles beyond the trail's end. Vistas to the north of the Saline River Valley are excellent. The summit elevation of Cave Hill is 923 feet above sea level. Retrace yours steps three miles back to the parking area.

Saline County State Fish & Wildlife Area is located between Harrisburg and Shawneetown, Illinois near the Saline and Gallatin County line. It is seven miles south of S.R. 13, five miles southwest of Equality and seven miles north of the Garden of the Gods entrance.

From I-24, take exit #14 onto U.S. 45 just north of Vienna, Illinois and drive about 30 miles northeast to Harrisburg Illinois and the junction of S.R. 13. From I-57, exit #54A-B east on S.R. 13 at Marion, Illinois and proceed to Harrisburg. Continue east from Harrisburg on S.R. 13 about ten miles to the junction with S.R. 142. Turn south and drive about a mile to Equality, Illinois. Turn south at the directional road sign south towards the Wildcat Hills. The gravel road route is well marked. Additional points of road access include following the directional signs from S.R. 145 about one mile south of Pankeyville, Illinois and from S.R. 34 just south of Rudement, Illinois heading to Stone Face.

This property is closed Christmas Day and New Year's Day.

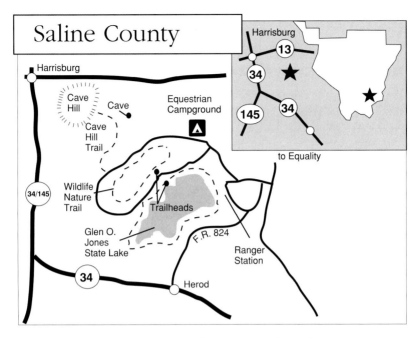

Saline County

Harrisburg

Harrisburg

Cave Hill   Cave
Cave Hill Trail

Equestrian Campground

to Equality

34/145

Wildlife Nature Trail

Trailheads

Glen O. Jones State Lake

F.R. 824

Ranger Station

34

Herod

Saline County Conservation Area

• • •

Location:
Equality, IL/Saline County

U.S.G.S. Map(s):
1:24,000 Rudement, Equality

Trail(s) Distance:
three trails total 6.75 miles

Acreage:
1,248 acres land and 105 acre lake

Activities:
hiking, nature study, picnicking,
shelters, playgrounds, fishing,
canoeing, boating, boat launch ramp,
boat rentals, seasonal hunting, bridle
trails, concessions

Fee(s):
rentals

• • •

Stone Face Recreation Site

Stone Face from above

*S*tone Face is an ancient geological limestone formation that appears to most viewers as an "old man's face" overlooking the Saline River Valley. The remote national forest hillside and blufftop hike is especially scenic and worth visiting.

*T*he trailhead begins where Forest Road 150 ends. Limited parking is available along the gravel shoulder at the loop. The limestone fine gravel trail forms a loop that heads uphill to the sandstone bluffs. A user-made trail leads west to the base of Stone Face which looks northward. Continue to follow the user path along the base of the bluff to a gap or access opening to the blufftop. Once on top, follow the bluff back left/east under the power lines. The blufftop becomes more scenic the closer you walk to Stone Face. The user trail skirts past barren rock, sandstone glades and undisturbed stands of blackjack oak and red cedar. This special place has been designated an Ecological Area by the Shawnee National Forest Service. There are several rock outcrops along the cliff but old Stone Face stands out among the rest. When winter snows cover Stone Face "he" even looks more weathered and ancient. Continue on along the blufftop to an obvious gap where you may descend to the original trail that leads back to the parking area.

*T*o reach Stone Face Recreation Site from I-24, take exit #16 east at Vienna on S.R. 147 and continue to the junction with S.R. 145 north of Glendale, Illinois. Go north on S.R. 145 to the junction with S.R. 34 just south of Mitchellsville, Illinois. Go east on S.R. 34 to the town of Rudement, Illinois. Follow the directional signs northeast about four miles along the gravel roads to Stone Face. Forest Road 150 is the entrance road and about a quarter mile long.

*F*rom I-57 exit #54 A-B east at Marion, Illinois on S.R. 13, proceed to Harrisburg, Illinois on S.R. 13 to the junction with S.R 45. Go south on S.R. 45 to the junction with S.R. 145/34 at the

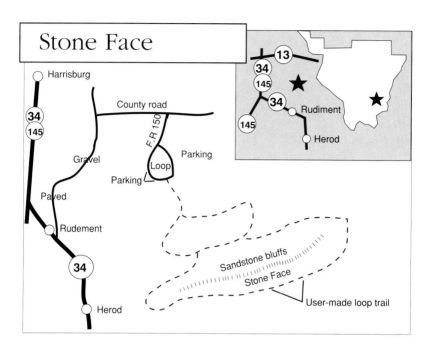

south edge of Harrisburg. Go south on S.R. 145/34 to the junction with S.R. 34 just past Mitchellsville. Go east on S.R. 34 to the town of Rudement. Follow the directional signs to Stone Face.

Stone Face Recreation Site

• • •

Location:
Rudement, IL/Saline County

U.S.G.S. Map(s):
1:24,000 Rudement

Trail(s) Distance:
one mile loop

Acreage:
60 acres

Activities:
nature hike, nature study, picnicking

Fee(s):
none

• • •

Rim Rock & Pounds Hollow Complex

Vista from Rim Rock Trail

*P*ounds Hollow was named after an Old English definition of "enclosures" or "impoundment" in reference to the prehistoric Late Woodland Indian (A.D. 600-800) rock wall at the entrance to Rim Rock, a 50 acre mesa-like tract "enclosed" on three sides by sandstone cliffs. Rim Rock is located upstream from Beaver Creek and Pounds Hollow Lake and Recreation Area. The 25 acre lake is nestled within a scenic valley surrounded by steep bluffs.

*T*he Rim Rock Forest Trail, a National Recreation Trail, encircles the escarpment on a 0.8 mile all-weather flagstone walk between the Indian Rock Wall picnic area and Pounds Hollow. The trail was constructed in 1963 by funds contributed by the Illinois Federation of Women. The Indian Wall may be seen at the trailhead entrance. It is believed the wall was built for defensive purposes when natural resources became scarce as populations grew. Pounds Hollow Lake may be seen from an opening in the forest at the top of the escarpment. A wooden stairway leading from an observation deck descends through narrow rock crevices known as "Fat Man's Misery" into lower Pounds Hollow and a huge rock shelter overhang called Ox-Lot Cave, a natural "corral" with springs utilized by early pioneers to contain farm animals. This latter-day enclosure also gives reinforcement to the place name "Pounds." Spring wildflowers are abundant on the forest floor of the hollow.

*T*he northwest terminus of the Beaver Trail is located to the immediate right of the Rim Rock Trailhead at Indian Wall picnic area. The Beaver Trail gradually descends the hollow about one-quarter mile to join with Lower Pounds Hollow Trail. Beaver Trail follows Beaver Creek downstream one-half mile along a gravel path to Pounds Hollow Lake beach and picnic area. The trail continues another one-half mile along the south shore to the dam and onto Camp Cadiz six miles away, the southeast terminus of Beaver Trail.

Hepaticas at Pounds Hollow

*Y*ou may continue to encircle Pounds Hollow Lake by continuing across the dam and following the undeveloped north shore around the 25 acre lake. The loop trail culminates near the base of Rim Rock in Pounds Hollow. Beaver activity is evident along the trail with fallen trees and a dam along the tributary creek. There is also a short spur that leads from Pine Ridge campground downhill to the beach and the trail.

*T*o reach Rim Rock & Pounds Hollow Recreation Complex from I-57, take exit #54A-B east onto S.R. 13 at Marion, Illinois and drive about 37 miles to the junction with S.R. 1. Turn south/right on U. S. 1 and proceed 8.6 miles to Karbers Ridge blacktop and turn west/right. Follow the road two miles to Pounds Hollow Recreation Area entrance and drive one mile to the beach and picnic area parking area. From Pounds Hollow entrance, drive one more mile west to the Rim Rock and Indian Wall picnic area entrance. The settlement of Karbers Ridge is located four miles west of the Recreation Complex. Follow the directional signs.

*F*rom I-24, take exit #16 east at Vienna, Illinois onto S. R. 146 and proceed to S.R. 34. Turn north onto S.R. 34 and continue to Karbers Ridge blacktop and turn east. Drive east past the community of Karbers Ridge to the national forest properties. You may also continue on S.R. 146 past Golconda, Illinois to S.R. 1 just north of Cave in Rock, Illinois. Go north on S.R. 1 about 12 miles to Karbers Ridge blacktop and turn left/west to the entrances.

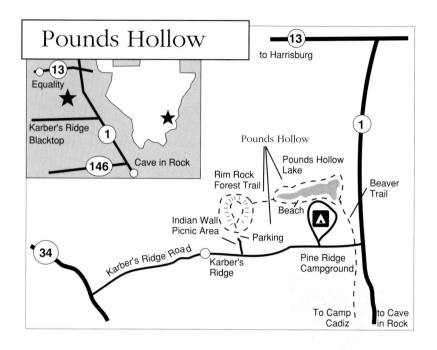

Rim Rock/Pounds Hollow Recreation Complex

• • •

Location:
Karbers Ridge, IL/Hardin County

U.S.G.S. Map(s):
1:24,000 Karbers Ridge

Trail(s) Distance:
approximately three and one-
quarter miles of trails

Activities:
hiking nature study, picnicking,
swimming (May 15–Sept 15),
bathhouse, lifeguard, fishing, non-
motorized boating, boat launch
ramp, campground (April–Dec 15),
concessions

Fee(s):
swimming, boat rentals, camping

• • •

High Knob Recreation Area

Vista from High Knob

*H*igh Knob is a 929 foot isolated hill of Pennsylvanian sandstone with vistas looking east towards Pounds Hollow and west to Garden of the Gods. The former fire observation tower site is rounded on top and makes an ideal picnic spot. A foot trail begins and ends on both sides of the access forest road at the entrance about 60 or 100 yards from the picnic and parking area. Although unmarked, the trail is well used and obvious. A rugged one mile loop trail follows the northwest side of the knob rim. Several other unmarked, short interconnecting loops are found in the High Knob Trail System. Short spurs connect southwest with the River-to-River Trail at the base of the knob downhill near the entrance.

*H*igh Knob Recreation Area is located between Garden of the Gods and Pounds Hollow just north of Karbers Ridge, Illinois. From I-24 at Vienna, take exit #16 east onto S.R. 146 and drive to Golconda, Illinois. Continue on S.R. 146 northeast to Humm Wye, Illinois and turn left/north on S.R. 34 and proceed to Karbers Ridge blacktop, south of Herod. Go east on the blacktop about five miles to Karbers Ridge, Illinois. At Karbers Ridge, turn north on F.R. 33, and go two miles and turn right/east. Go one more mile uphill to High Knob past a horse camp. Follow the directional signs. High Knob lies directly north of Karber's Ridge settlement. High Knob is mostly used during the day and is open from 6 a.m. to 10 p.m. Camping and leaving vehicles is permitted in the forest opening by the High Knob entrance that the River-to-River Trail passes through.

Dogwoods in bloom

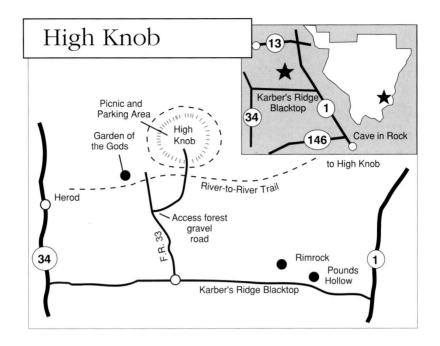

High Knob Observation & Picnic Area

• • •

Location:
Karbers Ridge, IL/Hardin County

U.S.G.S. Map(s):
1:24,000 Karbers Ridge

Trail(s) Distance:
several interconnecting trails total
two miles River-to-River Trail spur
access

Activities:
hiking, nature study, picnicking,
bridle trail access

Fee(s):
none

• • •

Garden of the Gods Recreation & Wilderness Area

Panoramic view at Garden of the Gods showing Camel Rock in lower left

6

Garden of the Gods features some of the most spectacular rock formations in the Illinois Ozark range. The eroding sandstone rocks are the remains of mountains that are 300 million years old. The area is located on the south side of an east-west trough formed by the northward tilt of the bedrock at this point, and has been greatly affected by earthquakes that are still taking place. The combined effects of tremors, glacial meltwaters, rain, freezing and thawing have naturally sculpted the bluffs into many and unusual formations such as Camel Rock, Devil's Smoke Stack, Table Rock, Chimney Rock, Anvil Rock, Mushroom Rock and Noah's Ark.

This recreation area is a special attraction and its popularity is resulting in over-use along its trails. The most popular trail is the quarter mile flagstone loop Observation Trail that begins and ends at the main parking lot. Camel Rock is the most outstanding formation along the easy cliffside path.

At the northwest end of the Observation Trail parking area is a wilderness forest trail leading to Anvil Rock, Shelter Rock, Mushroom Rock and Noah's Ark. Also on the northwest is River-to-River Trail access that continues four miles west to Herod and five miles east to High Knob and Camp Cadiz. You can spot the rock formation "Big H" as you hike the River-to-River Trail. The formation is not signed so remember to look up at the top of the bluffs.

Just beneath the formations and campground bluffs at the base of the hill are the lower trail spurs that also access the River-to-River Trail. An overnight parking area for Wilderness backpackers is available. An overgrown one mile linear trail leads out from the south end of the backpackers parking lot to Indian Point overlook. The surrounding trail segments total,

Mushroom Rock

Noah's Arc

Hiker on one of many rocks at Garden of the Gods

approximately five miles (excluding the River-to-River Trail). and offer several days or overnite hike loops and feeder spurs to the River-to-River Trail. Established in 1990 by an act of the U.S. Congress, 3,300 acres of the area is designated as the Garden of the Gods Wilderness Area. A topographical map or maps is recommended when exploring this area.

*T*o reach Garden of the Gods Recreation Area from I-24, take exit #16 east onto S.R. 146 at Vienna, Illinois and drive about 21 miles to Golconda Illinois on the Ohio River. Continue north on S.R. 146 to Humm Wye, Illinois and turn at the junction with S.R. 34 north. Proceed to Karbers Ridge blacktop, south of Herod. Go east on Karbers Ridge blacktop about four miles to F.H. 36. Continue north on F.H. 36 two miles to the entrance. The paved forest road winds upward around the base of the hills to the parking, picnicking and campground areas. Unless camping, the area is open 6 a.m to 10 p.m.

*F*rom I-57, take exit #54A-B and go east on S.R. 13 in Marion, Illinois and proceed to Harrisburg, Illinois. At Harrisburg, drive south on U.S. 45 at the intersection with S.R. 13. Go about two miles south on U.S. 45 to the junction with S.R. 34/145 then go five and one-half miles to Mitchellsville, Illinois and turn left on S.R. 34 towards Herod, Illinois. Continue south on S.R. 34 past Herod to Karbers Ridge blacktop. Go east on Karbers Ridge blacktop to F.H. 36 and turn north and drive two miles to the entrance. Just east of Garden of the Gods on Karbers Ridge blacktop is High Knob (four miles), Rim Rock National Recreation Trail and Indian Wall Picnic Area (six miles), Pounds Hollow Recreation Area (seven miles) and Camp Cadiz (nine miles). Continuing north from Garden of the Gods, about seven miles you will run into Saline County Conservation Area.

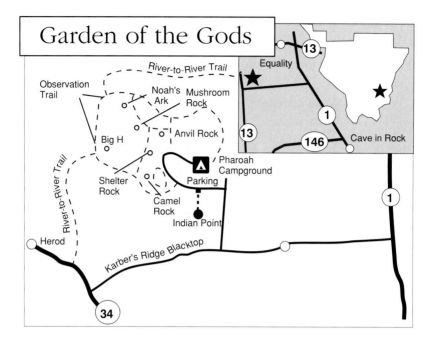

Garden of the Gods Recreation and Wilderness Area

• • •

Location:
Karbers Ridge, IL/Gallatin, County

U.S.G.S. Map(s):
1:24,000 Herod, Karbers Ridge

Trail(s) Distance:
Observation Trail 0.4 miles, Wilderness trails including River-to-River Trail total seven miles

Activities:
hiking, bridle trails, nature study, picnicking, campground, backcountry camping

Fee(s):
camping

• • •

Gibbons Creek Barrens

Glades at Gibbons Creek Barrens

*T*he Gibbons Creek Barrens area contains a network of trails and barrens that includes a sandstone glade and dry upland forest dominated by stunted oaks. The trails are well marked by eye-level blue blazes and posted signs. Although this trail is designated for disabled people, it is rugged and follows an old road bed and path that runs one-way along Gibbons Creek. The main trail is steep, rocky and rugged, encircling the preserve with side spur trails that lead to a spring, barrens and sandstone glades. Two shortcut trails divide the property.

*T*he barrens occupy a south slope that is a shrubby grassland of big and little bluestem Indian and June grasses. The dry, thin, rocky soil also supports several prairie flowering plants and old stunted trees of post, blackjack and black oaks. Occasional burns are prescribed to preserve the unique plant community. The sandstone glade is dominated by red cedars. Along the ridgetops there are scenic views to the West of Williams Hill, the second highest point in Illinois and Wamble Mountain to the North. Descending downhill, the portion of the trail along Gibbons Creek makes walking a pleasure.

*T*o reach Gibbons Creek Barrens from Vienna, Illinois and I-24, take exit #16 east onto S.R. 146 and drive 21 miles to Golconda, Illinois and continue northeast on S.R. 146 to Humm Wye, Illinois and the junction of S.R. 34. Go north on S.R. 34 about 10 to 12 miles to Herod, Illinois. From the post office in Herod continue on S.R. 34 for 1.3 miles to a gravel entrance road on the right side of the highway. Enter and proceed 0.2 miles to the small signed parking area and the trailhead. Please register at the mounted box. The preserve's hours are from 8 a.m. to 6 p.m.

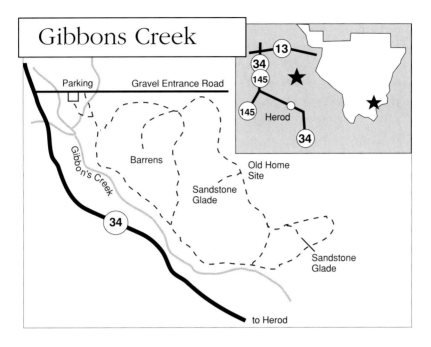

Gibbons Creek Barrens

• • •

Location:
Herod, IL. Pope County

U.S.G.S. Map(s):
1:24,000 Herod

Trail(s) Distance:
one and one-half miles

Activities:
nature walk, nature study, handicap
trail section

Fee(s):
none

• • •

Copperhead

Beaver Trail

The work of beavers at Pounds Hollow

*T*he Beaver Trail is a linear hike of seven easy to moderate miles one-way that begins or ends at Camp Cadiz (as does the River-to-River Trail). The trail heads northwest to end and/or begin at the Rim Rock National Recreation Trail next to Indian Wall Picnic Area. A marking system of white painted triangles appears at eye level on trees and other objects in both directions. The most difficult part of the trail is the distance especially in warm weather. Consider this hike in the spring or fall of the year.

*T*he trail follows a graveled forest road northwest from Camp Cadiz one and one-half miles to a cemetery. The trail curves around the graveyard along a dirt road path to enter a meadow 0.4 miles to where the trail narrows down to a path and enters a woods. The Beaver Trail then descends the wooded hillside zigzaging to descend the ridge and crossing two small streams, one of which is Beaver Creek. The distance hiked is two miles.

*T*he trail leads uphill from Beaver Creek through a revegetating meadow. The trail surface is now grassy and easy going through shortleaf pine plantations interspersed with prairie meadows of bluestem grasses and young woods. After a mile or so the trail comes to a tributary of Beaver Creek and crosses into a revegetating meadow. After a rain this section of the trail often fills with mud holes and is the most difficult place along the trail to hike. Across the meadow the trail changes direction heading northwest towards Pounds Hollow.

*T*his scenic woodland section includes a pleasant hike along the same stream you crossed before entering the meadow. Finally after a few tributary stream crossings, the trail heads uphill along an old road and joins an upland gravel road. Follow the gravel road about 300 yards to the left/west to Karbers Ridge blacktop crossing. Cross the road and enter a short-leaf pine plantation.

8

Trailhead at Rim Rock

You are now one mile from Pounds Hollow dam and two miles from Rim Rock and the end of the trail. Now the trail heads downhill to a ravine and small stream crossing and uphill through shortleaf pine plantations to reemerge into woodland and sandstone bluffs. Vistas of Pounds Hollow Lake come into view as the trail goes along the ridge to descend to the dam and around the lakeshore of the 25 acre lake to the beach. The trail continues through Pounds Hollow to Rim Rock and the Indian Wall picnic area, the northwest terminus of the Beaver Trail. Horse riders and an occasional ATV also use this trail.

*V*ehicles may be left overnight at Camp Cadiz in the mowed area immediately north of the camping area. Camping is permitted along any section of the trail until the Pounds Hollow Recreation Area is reached. Limited overnight parking is also available for several vehicles at Indian Wall Picnic Area near the north trailhead terminus next to the Rim Rock Trail.

A loop hike may be taken by continuing out of the Rim Rock Trail and Indian Wall Picnic Area by walking 100 yards south along the access road to Karbers Ridge blacktop/F.R. 17. Go right(west) and continue on the blacktop for about one mile to the intersection with F.R. 133. Go left/southeast and after approximately 0.1 miles at the McPherson-Love Cemetery entrance, go left/east and connect with the blue blazed River-to-River Trail. Continue on to Camp Cadiz. The additional four miles makes an 11 mile loop hike by road and trail. Due to the trail's distance you may consider a car shuttle from Camp Cadiz to Rim Rock and Indian Wall picnic area.

*T*o reach Camp Cadiz campground and the Beaver Trailhead south terminus from I-57, take exit 54 A-B east at Marion onto S.R. 13 and drive beyond Harrisburg, Illinois to the junction of

S.R. 13 and S.R. 1. Go south on S.R. 1 for 12 miles to C.R. 3 and turn right/west. Continue onto C.R. 4 about three miles to Camp Cadiz on the north side of the road.

*T*o reach Rim Rock National Recreation Trail at Indian Wall Picnic Area of Pounds Hollow Recreation Area from the crossroads of S.R. 13 and S.R. 1 go south about nine miles to Karbers Ridge blacktop F.R. 17 and drive west two and three miles to the access roads. From I-24 at Vienna, take exit #16 east onto S.R. 146 and drive to the junction of S.R. 1 north of Cave in Rock, Illinois. Go north to C.R. 4 about nine miles and follow the directional signs west to Camp Cadiz. It is 12 miles from the junction of S.R. 146 and S.R. 1 to Karbers Ridge blacktop, north of Cave in Rock, Illinois.

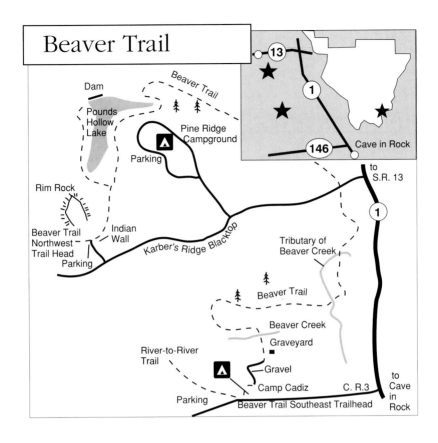

Beaver Trail

Dam

Pounds Hollow Lake

Beaver Trail

Pine Ridge Campground

Parking

Rim Rock

Beaver Trail Northwest Trail Head Parking

Indian Wall

Karber's Ridge Blacktop

13

1

146   Cave in Rock

to S.R. 13

1

Tributary of Beaver Creek

Beaver Trail

Beaver Creek

Graveyard

River-to-River Trail

Gravel

Camp Cadiz   C. R.3

Parking

Beaver Trail Southeast Trailhead

to Cave in Rock

Beaver Trail

• • •

Location:
Karbers Ridge, IL/Hardin County

U.S.G.S. Map(s):
1:24,000 Saline Mines, Karbers Ridge

Trail(s) Distance:
seven miles one-way

Activities:
hiking, nature study, backcountry camping

Fee(s):
none

• • •

The River-to-River Trail

One Horse Gap

Developed primarily as a horse trail but open to hiking, the River-to-River Trail is a rigorous four to eight day hike from Camp Cadiz, the eastern trail terminus (over 50 miles counting loops), to U.S. 45 highway about five miles north of Vienna, Illinois. Most nature walkers will prefer only the more scenic segments.

The longest hiking/horse trail in the Shawnee National Forest is maintained by the Elizabethtown District and the Vienna District. The main trail is marked by blue blazes in the Elizabethtown District and orange blazes in the Vienna District, although efforts are being made towards color consistency. The loop trails are located primarily in the Vienna District and are blazed in yellow, white, orange and red. The painted blazes appear at eye level on trees and other objects in both directions. The Elizabethtown section runs from Camp Cadiz to the area west of One Horse Gap on F.R. 120 and Concord Church south of Hartsville, Illinois. The Vienna section continues west from F.R. 120 to U.S. highway 45 near Taylor Church and Bluff. The latest trail segment to be completed is the 14.2 mile Camp Cadiz southeast to Battery Rock section. The national forest service is upgrading the trail and future plans will create new trail mileage that may one day truly provide a "River-to-River" pathway for equestrian riders and hikers. The proposed 127 mile trail will reach from Battery Rock on the Ohio River to Grand Tower on the Mississippi River. Some 30 miles are expected to follow county roads.

The hiker encounters a variety of terrain and vegetation types including wildlife openings and ponds, pine plantations, prairie glades, hardwood forests, hills, cliffs, outcrops, formations and streams. You can expect private property in the middle of the national forest so please respect it. The well-worn path

Tiger Swallow Tail Butterflies

utilizes hiking trails, dirt and gravel roads and one section of state highway near Herod, Illinois. Topographic maps are recommended. Camping is allowed on all parts of the trail bordered by national forest lands.

*F*rom the eastern terminus at Camp Cadiz, the River-to-River Trail winds west along F.R. 1715 to cross Karbers Ridge blacktop. The trail continues west and north along ridgetops and valleys to High Knob and onto the Garden of the Gods Wilderness Area then heads southwest to Herod, Illinois. The trail section northeast of Herod and High Knob is scenic with mature forest, rock formations, ridgetop vistas and hollows surrounded by towering bluffs. This is considered a popular segment to hike so don't expect to be alone on the weekends.

*W*hen you reach the town of Herod proceed north on S.R. 34 and cross the bridge and turn left/south on C.R. 146 and continue two and one-half miles until you cross the concrete dip. The trail goes southeast off C.R 146 uphill about three quarters of a mile to F.R. 186. Continue south on F.R. 186 to the forest trail leading to One Horse Gap. The River-to-River Trail will pick up and continue on F.R. 186 south to the junction with F.R. 1476. Go right/ northwest on F.R. 1476 to Concord Church. The trail does bypass the One Horse Gap area by going west on F.R. 1648 to the New Hope Church, south along C.R. 146 to Hartsville, Illinois and Concord Church or continuing northwest to Bethesda Church and F.R. 1816, dropping south to the East Fork of Little Lusk Creek.

*T*he trail winds west through Lusk Creek Wilderness Area and the trail junction to Lusk Creek Canyon Nature Preserve is another fine segment to hike. The main trail continues west and then south to Eddyville, Illinois. From Eddyville, the trail goes west along old forest service roads, fields and country roads north of Millstone Bluff Archeological Site, south of Jackson Hollow and around Cedar Creek or Trigg Observation Tower. At the F.R. 424 gravel road crossing and trail access, you will see a trail sign identifying several interconnecting loops between this point and U.S.45. They include:

> Max Creek Loop-Red Blaze–2.1 miles long
> Cedar Creek Loop-White Blaze–2.7 miles long
> E. Fork Cedar Creek Loop-Blue Blaze–one-half mile long

These loops appear to be less used by horsemen than the main trail. The River-to-River Trail's western terminus is on the east side of US. 45 about a quarter mile south of the Taylor Church and Cemetery.

To reach Camp Cadiz, the eastern terminus from I-57, take exit 54A-B east at Marion onto S.R. 13 and proceed towards Shawneetown, Illinois to the junction of S.R. 13 and S.R. 1. Go south on S.R. 1 about 12 miles (past Karbers Ridge blacktop about 3.5 miles) to C.R. 3. Take a right/west turn on C.R. 3 and drive about three miles to Camp Cadiz.

To reach the west terminus near Taylor Bluff from I-24, take exit #14 onto U.S. 45 at Vienna, drive north about four miles to the trailhead on the east side of the highway about one-quarter south of Taylor Church and Cemetery. A radio tower is as a helpful landmark. Other trail access points include: High Knob, Garden of the Gods, Herod, One Horse Gap, Lusk Creek Canyon, Eddyville, F.R. 423, F.R. 424 and U.S. 45.

Vehicles may be left overnight at most access points along federal, state, county and forest road crossings, however, it is best to park at supervised sites.

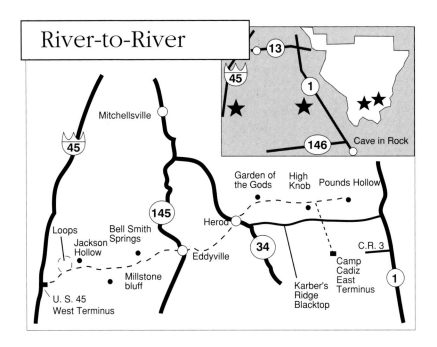

River-to-River

River-to-River Trail

• • •

Location:
Shawnee National Forest Vienna &
Elizabethtown Districts

U.S.G.S. Map(s):
1:24,000 Saline Mines, Karbers
Ridge, Herod, Eddyville,
Waltersburg, Stonefort, Glendale,
Bloomfield

Trail(s) Distance:
over 50 miles

Activities:
hiking, nature study, backcountry
camping, bridle trail, recreation
sites

• • •

9

Illinois Iron Furnace Recreation Site

Iron Furnace

*T*he Illinois Iron Furnace (1839-1883) was the first charcoal fired iron furnace in the Prairie State. During its heyday the 50 foot tall furnace generated enough iron pegs and ingots to support a community of 100 families in 1846. These families were mainly Irish from the East coast. During the Civil War (1861-1865) the turret-shaped' furnace was a principal supplier of iron for the Union ironclad ships and artillery. Local sources of charcoal, iron ore and limestone were hauled in and pig iron was hauled out by wagon to Elizabethtown, seven miles south, to be shipped down the Ohio River to a Union naval shipyard at Mound City, Illinois. The furnace was abandoned in 1883 when more economical methods and sources were discovered. At its peak production the daily output was around nine tons.

*T*he original iron furnace was dismantled for various construction projects. A facsimile was reconstructed on the former site in 1967. Its measurements are 42 feet high, 32 feet square at the base and 22 feet square at the top. The Illinois Iron Furnace was placed on the National Register of Historic Places in 1973.

*I*mmediately north of the Iron Furnace Historic Site is the Big Creek Trail, a one-half mile easy loop that begins and ends at the Iron Furnace picnic area. The pea gravel path follows the scenic stream along the floodplain forest. The undisturbed natural setting is good for birding. Sixteen miles of Big Creek is being recommended for study and possible inclusion in the National Wild and Scenic River System. The stream is a recognized natural zoological area. The river otter and the Indiana bat are rarely seen residents of Big Creek. Additional unmarked but obvious user trails are found in the adjacent area along the stream. Iron Furnace is a fine peaceful place to picnic and appreciate the historic past or take a short hike.

*T*o reach the recreation site from I-24, take exit #16 east onto S.R. 146 at Vienna, Illinois and drive about 35 miles to Elizabethtown, Illinois. The recreation area is located about seven miles north of Elizabethtown and S.R. 146, and four miles north of Rosiclare, Illinois and seven miles south of Karbers Ridge, Illinois. Follow the directional signs

*I*n addition, just southeast of Iron Furnace are two man-made lakes that offer fishing, non-motorized boating, carry-down boat launch ramps and non-developed dispersed camping. Lake Tecumseh lies north of Whoopie Cat Lake and both are about three miles north of Elizabethtown. Fishermen paths encircle the small bodies of water.

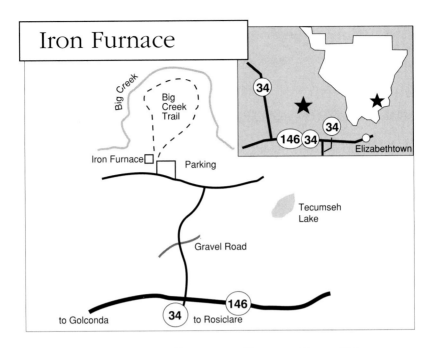

Illinois Iron Furnace Recreation Site

• • •

Location:
Elizabethtown, IL/Hardin
County

U.S.G.S. Map(s):
1:24,000 Rosiclare

Trail(s) Distance:
one-half mile loop

Activities:
nature walk, nature study,
historic site, picnicking,
shelters, recreational playfields,
fishing, primitive camping at
nearby Whoopee Cat Lake &
Lake Tecumseh

Fee(s):
none

10

Tower Rock Recreation Area

Tower Rock

*T*ower Rock is one-hundred and sixty feet high and is the highest point on the Ohio River. No other natural point along this significant stream from Pittsburgh, Pennsylvania to Cairo, Illinois is higher. No doubt the historic landmark served as a lookout as long as humans have occupied the area. According to local historians, the Shawnee utilized the lookout point to observe the steady influx of American settlers who were making the Ohio River valley their home. The majestic vista from the overlook is worth the short forest hike uphill along graveled switchbacks. The trail begins east of the boat launch and parking area. The trail is in good condition and is approximately one-eighth mile long.

A longer unmarked woodland path may be hiked beginning adjacent to the main paved entry road at the hillcrest before it descends steeply to the river. The old forest or wildlife road penetrates the mature deciduous forest. One spur leads downridge north to access the county river road.

*F*rom May 1 to December 15, excellent shaded riverside terrace camping is available in the 35 level campsites. Other amenities include picnicking, grills, garbage disposal, pit toilets, pump water and a concrete boat launch ramp. A small grove of pecan trees grows here.

*T*o reach Tower Rock Recreation Area from I-24, take exit #16 east onto S.R. 146 at Vienna and drive to Elizabethtown, approximately 42 miles. Follow the directional signs northeast of Elizabethtown, past the Elizabethtown Ranger District Office, on S.R. 146 and turn right/east on River Road. Continue to the entrance about four miles. Tower Rock Recreation Area is located about seven miles east of Elizabethtown and four miles west of Cave in Rock along River Road.

Gar and Turtle on the shoreline

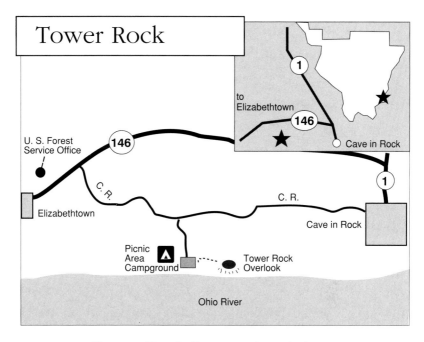

Tower Rock

T o w e r   R o c k   R e c r e a t i o n a l   A r e a

• • •

Location:
Elizabethtown, IL/Hardin County

U.S.G.S. Map(s):
1:24,000 Cave in Rock

Trail(s) Distance:
0.25 miles

Activities:
nature walk, nature study,
picnicking, boating, boat launch
ramp, camping (May 1–Dec 15)

Fee(s):
camping

• • •

Cave in Rock State Park

View to the entrance of Cave in Rock

*T*he Ohio riverside state park may be small in acreage but big on facilities and activities. Cave in Rock is also rich in historical fact, lore and legend. In 1729, two centuries before becoming an Illinois state park, the Ohio River bluffside limestone cave was visited by Frenchmen M. deLery who named it, *Caverne dans le Roc,* or "Cave in Rock." Prior to European discovery, the cave was a center of Indian life.

*T*he famous landmark of Ohio River travelers became the base of infamous operations for numerous bands of pirates during the Revolutionary War and until about 1834. Once a tavern and inn, desperadoes such as the infamous Harpe brothers would lure innocent passersby to the cave to be robbed and killed. Early travelers were forewarned by the guidebook, "The Navigator," to beware of Ohio River outlaws near the notorious cave.

*T*he unique cave's exterior is flushed flat against the east face of a tall limestone bluff. The arched mouth measures 55 feet wide. Easily accessed by foot and occasionally by canoe during high water, the interior measures 40 feet high and 160 feet long. There are fine vistas of the Ohio River especially during sunrise. The movies, "How the West Was Won" and Walt Disney's "Davy Crockett and the River Pirates" feature scenes of Cave in Rock as well as Battery Rock, the future east terminus of the River-to-River Trail, located upstream a few miles east of Lamb, Illinois. Cave in Rock is a short 200 yard walk from the parking area along the main park road next to the playground.

*T*he three-fourth mile Hickory Ridge Loop Trail skirts the lodge, campground and picnic area. The woodland trail traverses ravine bottoms and tree-covered uplands. The trailhead begins and ends just west of the restaurant along the main park road near the tent campground.

View of the Ohio River

*T*he three-fourth mile Pirate Bluff Trail begins at the east end of the cabin lodge parking area next to the restaurant. The trailhead is marked. Follow the path downhill to a river ravine and sandy cove. The trail ascends the ravine on a south facing wooded slope and emerges along the main park road. Exercise caution when crossing the road to the meadow beyond. The trail curves through the field to enter a woods and descends to join the Hickory Ridge Loop Trail. Go left to return to the restaurant or go right to the campground.

*T*o reach Cave In Rock State Park from I-24, take exit #16 east onto S.R. 146 at Vienna, Illinois and drive about 50 miles to the junction of S.R 1. Turn south on S.R 1 and continue two miles to the community of Cave in Rock. Turn east at the town center on New State Park Road and drive one-half miles to the park entrance. The park borders the Ohio River for about a mile. The only Illinois ferry service on the Ohio River shuttles cars and passengers across the river from the town center into Kentucky, accessing KY S.R. 135 and U.S. 91.

*F*rom I-57, take exit #54A-B east onto S.R. 13 at Marion, Illinois and drive approximately 35 miles to the junction with S.R. 1, sixteen miles west of Shawneetown, Illinois. Turn south on S.R. 1 and drive 21 miles to Cave in Rock. Follow the directional signs east along the river to the park entrance.

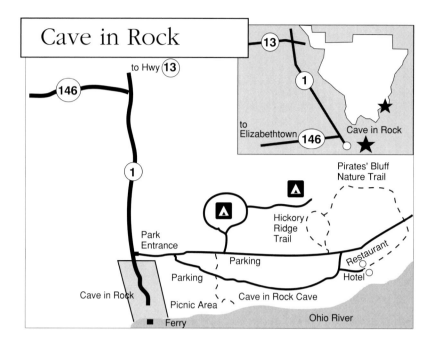

Cave in Rock State Park

• • •

Location:
Cave in Rock, IL/Hardin County

U.S.G.S. Map(s):
1:24,000 Cave in Rock

Trail(s) Distance:
two trails total one and one-half
miles

Acreage:
200 acres

Activities:
nature trails, nature study, picnicking,
shelters, playground, river boating,
boat launch ramps, fishing, trout
pond, cabin lodge, restaurant, class B
& C campgrounds, concessions

Fee(s):
camping, lodge, shelter reservations

• • •

Tower Rock on the Ohio River (Walk #11)

Vienna District

Lusk Creek Canyon Nature Preserve

Indian Kitchen at Lusk Creek Canyon

*L*usk Creek Canyon at Indian Kitchen area is considered by many to be the most scenic natural area in southern Illinois. The canyon was dedicated in 1970 as a state nature preserve to protect its botanic, zoologic, geologic, historic and native beauty. The 100 foot-high canyon was carved by Lusk Creek through layers of Pennsylvanian sandstone bedrock. The nature preserve is surrounded by the 4,796 acre Lusk Creek Wilderness Area of the Shawnee National Forest and is easily accessed by walking the vehicle-wide service roads. The diverse topography and geological features include flat ridgetops, steep ravines, sinkholes, sandstone canyons, shelter caves and stream terraces

*T*he easy to rugged Indian Kitchen Trail is a linear hike that begins across the road from the small graveled parking lot at the metal gate and registration box. Hikers be advised the clay path can be slick when wet. Horses and an occasional ATV also use the trail. The trail passes by an old home site and open pasture then enters into continuous shortleaf pine plantations on both sides to eventually descend into the canyon one and one-quarter miles later. The Illinois Division of Natural Heritage has established a registration box for canyon visitors to sign in.

*T*he hike into the canyon is three-fourths mile and is considered difficult, especially when wet. Sugar maple, beech and tulip trees comprise the dominant woody species of the valley floor while white oak and red oak predominate on the slope. The dry blufftops support blackjack oak, post oak and scarlet oak. The path narrows as it descends into the majestic gorge and culminates at the creek's edge. The stream forms a hair pin turn and the huge canyon wall is amphitheater-shaped. The stream is popular with canoeists. The Indian Kitchen area of the nature preserve has been designated a National Natural Landmark.

13

White Water at Lusk Creek

The "Kitchen" refers to the rock shelter that was occupied by the Late Woodland Indians (600-900 A.D.) at the canyon's northeast shelf. Over 800 species of ferns and flowering plants thrive here and over 100 bird species have been counted. Rare northern plants survive along the rocky ledge of the canyon such as Turks cap lily, hay scented fern and arching dewberry. You must retrace your steps along the original path to the parking lot. If you continue northwest on the unmarked trail instead of descending into the canyon, it will connect the River-to-River Trail in about a mile. This is a popular area with horsemen.

Lusk Creek Canyon Nature Preserve is four miles northeast of Eddyville, Illinois. From I-24, take exit #16 at Vienna, Illinois and go east onto S.R. 147 through Simpson, Illinois and Robbs, Illinois to the S.R. 145 junction. Go left/northeast on S.R. 145 to Eddyville and turn right/east onto C.R. 5, the blacktop to Golconda. Follow the blacktop 1.4 miles from Eddyville, turn left on the first gravel road C.R. 126 and continue about one and one-half miles to the marked parking area on the west side of the road. The trailhead is located directly across the road from the parking lot. For further information contact the Site Superintendent at Saline County Conservation Area, Equality, Illinois.

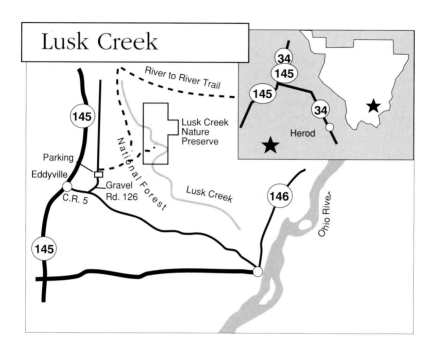

Lusk Creek

River to River Trail

145

Lusk Creek Nature Preserve

National Forest

Parking

Eddyville

Gravel Rd. 126

C.R. 5

Lusk Creek

146

Ohio River

34

145

145

34

Herod

145

13

Lusk Creek Canyon Nature Preserve

• • •

Location:
Eddyville, IL/Pope County

U.S.G.S. Map(s):
1:24,000 Eddyville

Trail(s) Distance:
two miles one-way, also River-to-
River trail access

Acreage:
125 acre state preserve surrounded
by Shawnee National Forest

Activities:
hiking, nature study

Fees:
none

• • •

Bell Smith Springs Recreation Area

Teal Pond

*M*ost forest visitors would agree Bell Smith Springs is one of the most outstanding nature sites in southern Illinois and the Shawnee National Forest. Hunting Branch, Mill Branch, Bay Creek and Spring Branch have carved numerous rock formations and deep canyons into the Pennsylvanian sandstone. Special natural features include the springs, gaps, cliffs, boulder strewn streams, a grist mill site and a 125 foot long, 30 foot-high natural bridge. According to botanist Robert H. Mohlenbrock, 20% of the flowering plants and ferns found in Illinois are growing at the site. The recreation area is noted for its abundance of spring wildflowers. The name is derived from an early 19th century pioneer property owner, Bell Smith. Bell was his mother's maiden name.

*F*our maintained hiking trails that total over eight miles distance loop and interconnect along the ridges and canyon bottoms. The General Area Hiking Trail or White Trail is 1.4 miles in length and is marked by white diamonds on trees at eye level and rocks at ground level. The trail begins and ends at the Hunting Branch picnic area and explores the upper bluffs and canyons southeast of the picnic area leading past the Devil's Backbone, down the carved steps to Bay Creek, past the springs and back to the picnic area. Swimming and wading in Bay Creek is a popular summertime activity.

*T*he Sentry Bluff Trail or Blue Trail is 3.2 miles and is marked by blue diamonds. The trail begins and ends near the dead end parking area of F.R. 848. The longest trail at Bell Smith Recreation Area leads along the blufftops of Bay Creek, crossing Bay Creek, continuing on to Sentry Bluff and Boulder Falls and eventually Natural Bridge. Be careful when crossing Bay Creek during higher than normal water because of

Natural Bridge at Bell Smith Springs

the slick algae-covered rocks. The trail loops back descending the canyon at Fox Gap and the natural bridge to Bay Creek and ascends the canyon back to the trailhead. Jay and Chute Gaps lead to the Bay Creek canyon from the blufftop trail. Owl Gap leads from Redbud campground downhill to the Sentry Bluff Trail.

*T*he Natural Bridge Trail or Yellow Trail is a one and one-half mile loop that also begins and ends at the parking lot dead end of F.R. 848. As the name suggests, the trail leads from the parking lot to Jay Gap, Bay Creek and the Natural Bridge to return to the parking lot. It is believed the amazing span of sandstone "bridge" was at one time a bluff shelter and will probably remain intact until the end supports erode away.

*T*he fourth trail is the Mill Branch Trail or Orange Trail which is marked with orange blazes. The two mile scenic trail begins and ends at Hunting Branch picnic area following the upper bluffs of Mill Branch. The location of a pioneer gristmill may be seen along the two mile Mill Branch Loop. The scenic stream bed has been sculpturesquely carved by water erosion.

*O*riginally the Shawnee Hills Hikers planned to blaze the Heritage Hiking Trail. This unfinished 60 mile loop backpacking-hiking trail would have connected Bell Smith Springs, Teal Pond and Burden Falls, north to Murray Bluff east to S.R. 145, south to William's Hill, Lusk Creek and west to the River-to-River Trail and finally north to Jackson Hollow and Bell Smith Springs. The Burden Falls Trail section is blazed along the south bluff bank and serves to guide those who want to get a closer look at the seasonal 100 foot falls from the lower stream bed. Burden Falls is accessed at F.R. 402 about four miles west of the junction with S.R. 145 at Delwood, Illinois. Burden Falls Wilderness access

Bay Creek

sites are located at F.R. 447 about one and one-third miles west of the junction with S.R. 145 and F.R. 447 about 3.6 miles west of the junction with S.R. 145.

*T*o reach the Bell Smith Springs Recreation Area, Teal Pond campground and Burden Falls from I-24 at Vienna, Illinois, take exit #16 east onto S.R. 147 and drive northeast through Simpson, Illinois and Robbs, Illinois to the junction of S.R. 145. Turn left/east on S.R. 145, continue north through Eddyville 2.5 miles to F.R. 447 and go west three and one-half miles to the junction with F.R. 848 and Teal Pond. Turn south on F.R. 848 from F.R. 447 and drive one and one-half miles to Hunting Branch picnic area, Redbud campground and eventually the dead-end circular drive and parking lot trailhead.

*Y*ou may also continue north on S.R. 145 to Delwood and turn west on F.R. 402. Drive six miles to the junction with F.R. 447, turn left and proceed two miles to the junction with F.R. 848 at Teal Pond. Turn south on F.R. 848 and drive to Bell Smith Springs Recreation Area.

*T*o reach Burden Falls from Teal Pond campground go one and one-third miles northwest on F.R. 447 to the road fork and F.R. 402 and turn right/east onto F.R. 402 and continue one-half mile to the road ford dip and the small parking area on the left side of the road. Burden Falls is just west of the parking area.

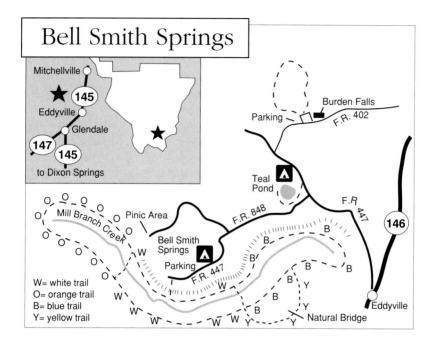

Bell Smith Springs

Mitchellville

★ 145

Eddyville

Glendale

147 145

to Dixon Springs

Burden Falls

Parking

F.R. 402

Teal Pond

F.R. 447

146

Mill Branch Creek

Pinic Area

F.R. 848

Bell Smith Springs

Parking

F.R. 447

W= white trail
O= orange trail
B= blue trail
Y= yellow trail

Eddyville

Natural Bridge

14

Bell Smith Springs Recreation Area

• • •

Location:
Eddyville, IL/Pope County

U.S.G.S. Map(s):
1:24,000 Stonefort

Trail(s) Distance:
four interconnecting trails total
approximately eight miles

Activities:
hiking, nature study, picnicking,
swimming, fishing, camping

Fee(s):
camping

• • •

Jackson Hollow

Rappellers at Jackson Hollow

*J*ackson Hollow was named after Orange Jackson, one of the first settlers in the area. The sheer cliffs, shelter bluffs, caves, tunnels, rock formations and waterfalls are interesting to explore year-round. Rare ferns such as walking and filmy ferns survive on shaded north exposures of limestone cracks and crevices along the bluff.

*T*o reach this national forest site from F.R. 424 requires about three-fourths to one mile hike east along old Forest Road 1770 through shortleaf pine plantations and forest borders. Jackson Hollow will be on your left/north side as you hike, but access is difficult due to the steep sandstone bluffs. At the end of the F.R. 1770 hike you will come to the Illinois Central railroad tracks and Little Bay Creek. Little Bay Creek and tributaries have cut through the canyon providing access to the difficult terrain. ATV's have cut an obvious path alongside the creek that leads upstream to the main features of the hollow. The ATV path leads uphill to the private property of Day's Horse Rides and the main F.R. 424. Be sure to bring a topographical map to locate the rock formations that are so outstanding in Jackson Hollow. Some explorers actually rappel into the hollow.

*T*hree side hollows to explore in addition to Jackson Hollow are Wildcat, Brown's and Cove. Special features of these hollows include Dripping Rock Spring, Turkey Pen Gap, Brown's Hollow gorge and numerous rock formations. The intrusive Illinois Central Railroad divides Jackson Hollow north and south. There are just as many exciting "streets" to explore on both sides of the railroad embankment. It would be easy to spend an entire day in the hollow.

*T*o reach Jackson Hollow from I-24, take exit #16 east onto S.R. 146 at Vienna and drive one-third mile to S.R. 147.

Balanced Rock

Travel about eight miles northeast to Simpson, Illinois. Go north on F.R. 424 just east of the post office in Simpson. Enroute to the Trigg Observation Tower (located three miles from Simpson) you will see the Simpson Township's Barrens on the right side of the road and a pull out. The Shawnee National Forest Service has placed an interpretive sign explaining the flora, fauna and life cycle of the prairie sandstone barrens or glades. Continue north 2.6 miles past the climbable Trigg and Cedar Creek firetower (good views of Millstone Bluff, east) and the River-to-River Trail crossing. At this point, F.R. 1770 will be on your right and appears like an old farm lane. Day's Horse Rides parking grassy area will be on your left and a wood sided house will be adjacent north of the access hiking route. You may park alongside the gravel road and walk the old F.R. 1770 about a mile east to the railroad tracks, Little Bay Creek and Jackson Hollow.

*J*ackson Hollow lies north of Simpson and Robbs, Illinois near the Pope and Johnson County line and ten miles west of Eddyville off McCormick Road.

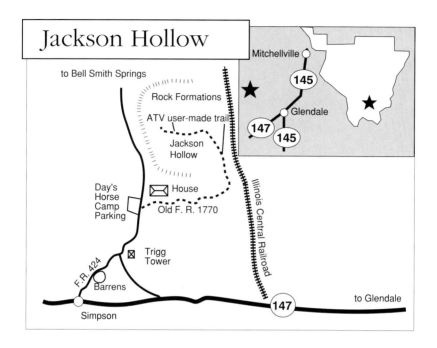

Jackson Hollow

• • •

Location:
Robbs, IL/Pope County

U.S.G.S. Map(s):
1:24,000 Stonefort

Trail(s) Distance:
unmarked, 4-5 miles total

Acreage:
289 acres

Activities:
hiking, nature study, rappelling

Fee(s):
none

• • •

Millstone Bluff Archeological Site

Thunderbird in rock at Millstone Bluff

*M*illstone Bluff features one of the best preserved Indian rock carvings or petroglyphs in North America and the Middle West. The 700 foot isolated knob rises nearly 320 feet above the surrounding valley of Bay Creek between the communities of Robbs and Glendale, Illinois. The wooded blufftop is composed of a three acre, level sandstone caprock. Prehistoric native American cultures such as the Paleo, Archaic, Woodland and Mississippian utilized the area for about 10,000 years.

*T*he interpretive trail leads uphill from the old quarry parking lot along a forest path to the bluff top through a wooden staircase. The short but invigorating walk leads visitors to a prehistoric stone wall, rock carvings, a former village and plaza. Archeological evidence reveals the prominent hill was a significant ceremonial center. Interpretive stations provide a wealth of information and illustration about Millstone Bluff's past. The place name Millstone is derived from the Euro-American pioneers who quarried the sandstone around the bluff to produce millstones to grind corn. The national forest service developed the archeological-historical site in 1991. Please stay on the path to protect the fragile area for future generations.

*P*hysical evidence has revealed the Woodland Indians were the first occupants of the site before the Mississippians. The Woodland people lived in temporary small family camps and were non-agricultural relying on wild plants and wild game. A six foot-wide and high stone fence or fort was erected for protection against warring groups. There are ten other stone fort sites scattered across southern Illinois including Giant City State Park, where a trail leads to an actual fort and stone wall.

*S*everal hundred years later the Mississippian's occupied the bluffs, building rectangular permanent houses and growing crops like corn, beans, squash and tobacco. A plaza or public square was developed near the village center in a flat area where today few trees grow in the compact soil. Midway, at the west edge of the boardwalk overlook, an overhanging rock outcrop displays rock carvings of a thunder bird and spider spirits. These animals were thought to possess spirits and were given offerings and prayer. Additional petroglyphs found at Millstone Bluff include a bear's paw, an eagle, peace pipes, a cross with a circle, a sun wheel, an elbow pipe and a corn plant.

*H*igh infant mortality was common. The average life-span of an average person was in the 30's and senior citizens were considered to be fifty years-old. Each person and family were buried separately and in different positions. The blufftop Mississippian population was estimated to be about one-hundred at its cultural peak. Approximately 900 years ago the site was abandoned. Millstone Bluff is listed as a National Historic Site.

*T*o reach Millstone Bluff from I-24, take exit #16 at Vienna, Illinois and drive east 0.3 miles onto S.R. 146 and turn left/north on S.R 147. Drive about ten miles to the entrance, located one mile east of Robbs at F.R. 532 on the north side of the highway. Enter F. R. 532 and drive one-third mile to the dead end parking area at the old quarry and the trailhead. A porta-john is available but no water.

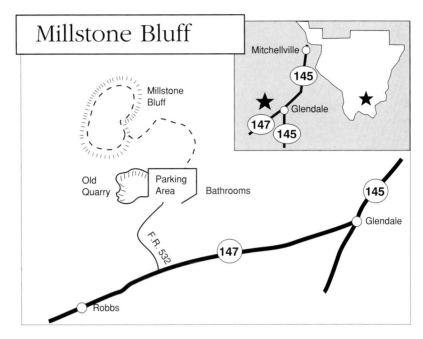

Millstone Bluff Archeological Site

• • •

Location:
Robbs, IL/Pope County

U.S.G.S. Map(s):
1:24,000 Glendale

Trail(s) Distance:
one-half mile loop

Acreage:
258 acres

Activities:
interpretive hike, nature study,
archeological & historic site

Fee(s):
none

• • •

16

Lake Glendale Recreational Area

Crayfish tower at Lake Glendale

Scenic Lake Glendale was formed from a tributary of Sugar Creek. The national forest facility is a developed recreational area easily accessed from S.R. 145 south of Glendale, Illinois and Dixon Springs Agricultural Center. The popular recreational site includes an 80 acre lake ideally suited for swimming, non-motorized boating and fishing. Two three-mile marked loop trails provide opportunities for visitors to stretch their legs and see the surrounding terrain.

The well marked and maintained Lake Glendale Trail encircles the shoreline of the serene lake that was constructed in the late 1930's. The gravel path encircles the lake with access points located at Duck Bay, Goose Bay, Pine Point Picnic Area and Oak Point Campgrounds on the south side of the lake. The beach and picnic area on the north side also provides trail access. A short loop trail encircles the Illinois Federation of Women Club's short-leaf pine plantation between Cardinal Bay boat launch and Goose Bay Picnic Area.

The Signal Point Trail begins and ends south of the Duck Bay picnic area where parking is available. The blazed path leads through forest and field five-eighths mile to Signal Point bluff. The loop trail follows the base of the bluff in both directions and continues uphill to follow the ridge and its dry glade community and return to the trail entry point at the base of Signal Point. Supposedly the bluff was a signaling point during the Civil War to relay information and an old stagecoach road between Golconda and Vienna is found in the area that was also the route of the Trail of Tears. Return to Duck Bay along the original five-eighths mile forest trail or the optional return route along an inlet tributary. Hikers be aware that horse riders also share this trail, especially along the base and on top of the Signal Point bluff.

"Looking up"

To reach Lake Glendale Recreation Area from I-24, take exit #16 east at Vienna Illinois onto S.R. 146 and drive 11 miles to the intersection ramp of S.R. 145 and Dixon Springs State Park. Go north on S.R. 145, two miles to the recreation area entrance.

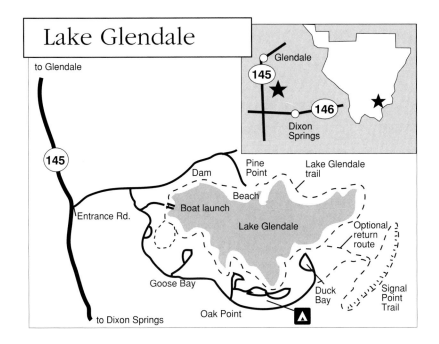

Lake Glendale Recreation Area

• • •

Location:
Shawnee National Forest,
Glendale, IL/Pope County

U.S.G.S. Map(s):
1:24,000 Glendale

Trail(s) Distance:
two trails total six and one-half
miles

Activities:
hiking, nature study, picnicking,
shelters, lake swimming, lifeguards,
bathhouse, non-motorized boating,
boat launch, pier fishing, camping,
concessions, handicapped access

Fee(s):
boat rental, camping

• • •

Dixon Springs State Park

Spring House at Dixon Springs

*D*ixon Springs was named in honor of William Dixon, one of the first pioneers to settle in the area. Prior to Euro-American settlement, the area was known by the Shawnee Indians as, "Kitche-mus-ke-nee-be," or "Sacred Medicine Waters." The tiny community of Dixon Springs became established with a general store, post office, blacksmith shop, gristmill and several churches. During the 19th century, the healthful healing waters of seven springs at Dixon Springs were commercialized into a health spa. Today the churches still remain at the former village site within the park boundary. One roof-covered spring still flows pure from a fractured fault line if you need healthful water.

*R*ock formations are outstanding features of the park. Outcrops, overhangs and cliffs bear such names as Album Rock, Red Man's Retreat, Wolf Pen, Lover's Leap, Pluto's Cave, Alligator Rock, The Chain of Rocks, Devil's Workshop and Honey Comb Rock.

*T*hree easy nature trails: Pine Tree, Bluff and Oak Tree all loop and interconnect, forming one trail that is 1.7 miles long. Pine Tree Trail leads through a short leaf pine plantation. The linear, vehicle-wide, grassy path begins near the upland picnic shelter, east of the churches. Pine Tree Trail connects with Bluff Trail. The shaded forest path leads past rock overhang shelters and outcrops and connects with Oak Tree Trail, passing through a regenerating meadow. A large white oak appears along the trail giving rise to the trail's name. Oak Tree Trail skirts the site superintendent's office and eventually interconnects with Pine Tree Trail and the original trailhead.

*R*ecently established, Ghost Dance Canyon Trail is a three-quarter mile loop leading exploring hikers down Hill Branch and back on top and along the east canyon wall. The scenic but rugged path begins south of the swimming pool parking area, leading under S.R. 146 arch bridge to the canyon. Boulder breakdown fills the narrow stream bed. Caution should be used when crossing the stream on slippery rocks. The trail heads uphill to the blufftop and back to the bridge and parking lot.

*T*o reach Dixon Springs State Park from I-24, take exit #16 east onto S.R. 146 at Vienna, Illinois and drive approximately 11 miles to the park entrance on the north side of the highway just beyond the junction of S.R. 146 and S.R. 145. Dixon Springs is about ten miles west of Golconda, Illinois.

*L*ike most state facilities, the park is open year around except Christmas Day and New Year's Day.

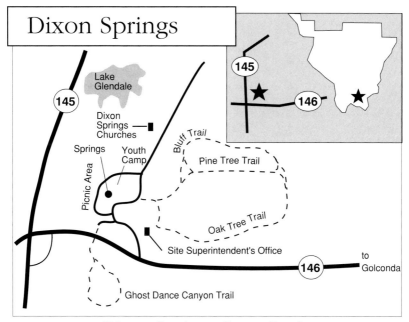

Dixon Springs State Park

• • •

Location:
Dixon Springs, IL/Pope County

U.S.G.S. Map(s):
1:24,000 Glendale

Trail(s) Distance:
four trails total approximately two and
one-half miles

Acreage:
596 acres

Activities:
hiking, nature study, picnicking,
shelters, play grounds, ball fields, pool
swimming, lifeguard, bathhouse, Class
B trailer camping, cabins and primitive
campground, concessions

Fee(s):
swimming, rentals, camping, cabins

• • •

18

Wildcat Bluff & Little Black Slough

Ford at Cache River to Boss Island

*T*his portion of the vast 9,200 acre Cache River Natural Area provides access to two maintained hiking trails in the northern portion of Little Black Slough. The State of Illinois with the assistance of The Nature Conservancy purchased the tract during the 1970s and about half of the natural area is dedicated as an Illinois Nature Preserve. Little Black Slough harbors cypress and tupelo swamps, low floodplain forests, upland forests, dry blufftop woods and hillside barrens. Two nature trails begin and end at the dead-end turn-around, next to a farm house at Wildcat Bluff where there is limited parking.

*L*ook Out Point Trail is a one mile easy trail that heads east at the closed metal gate and follows an old road along the level forested ridgetop to end at a sandstone outcrop overlooking the Cache River bottoms. Much of the dry upland forest of Wildcat Bluff escaped cutting for timber due to the fact they were often gnarly or hollow in response to the adverse growing conditions. There are great views of the bottomlands and beyond when the leaves are down. This linear trail requires retracing your steps back to the parking lot.

*L*ittle Black Slough Trail is a six and one-half mile partial loop that heads west at the opposite closed metal gate. Leading west one mile along Wildcat Bluff, the old road trail descends into the Cache River floodplain forest and follows the bank another half mile to a rock ford across the Cache River. Historically the French "Black Robes" Mermet and St. Denis who discovered the river for France, named the stream Cache or "hidden" because of the difficulty in locating it. Modern day hikers may have difficulty fording the stream during rainy weather until a permanent bridge is constructed, however, the task of crossing is part of the adventure.

Cypress knees

*O*nce across the Cache River you are on Boss Island, a large tract of upland surrounded by Little Black Slough. The place name Boss is a corruption of "Bost," a family of early settlers on the island. A settlement known as Scalin Spur once existed on Boss Island during the early 1900s. The trail intersects an active railroad crossing and an old homestead before the loop junction.

*G*o left at the loop junction where the vehicle-wide trail leads through sycamore, tulip poplar and pine plantations to a sandstone bluff that overlooks Little Black Slough. The trail follows the sandstone forested bluff for some distance before looping back north. As the trail curves back north, an old forest road goes straight along the bluff to the western tip of Boss Island where old growth trees are evident, especially in the "shoreline" area between the slough and the bluff. Retrace your steps back to the trail loop and continue north.

*T*he loop trail will curve east heading back to the Cache River crossing. At this point a second spur trail heads out to the western tip of Boss Island that is hikeable and again you must retrace your steps. The remainder of the loop trail passes through tree plantations and offers little scenery. Continue to cross the river and head uphill back to the Wildcat Bluff parking area. Although the trail is obvious, it is blue-blazed.

*T*o reach Wildcat Bluff access parking area from I-24, take exit #16 west at Vienna onto S.R. 146 and drive about six miles to Wildcat Bluff Road on the south side of the highway about one-half mile from West Vienna and the junction of S.R. 146 and S.R. 37. The parking area and trailhead are about six miles south of S.R. 146. You may also turn south at the junction of S.R. 146 and U.S. 45 at Vienna. Take U.S. 45 south 2.8 miles to a gravel road and turn right/west. Follow the directional signs to Wildcat Bluff, another three miles from the turn.

*F*rom I-57, take exit 30 east onto S.R. 146 and drive about nine miles to West Vienna. The access road is about one-half mile east of the crossroads S.R. 37 and S.R. 146. Follow the directional signs for six miles to Wildcat Bluff.

A third entry point, the North Cypress Access Area, may be reached from S.R. 37 south of West Vienna and north of Cypress, but does not have any hiking trails and is designed for hunter access as are the other access sites of Forman, Belknap and Marshall Ridge. For further information contact the site superintendent at Cache River Natural Area Headquarters at Belknap, Illinois.

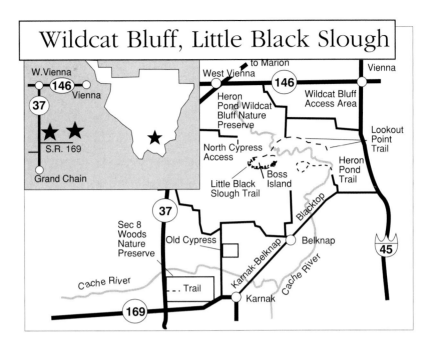

Wildcat Bluff & Little Black Slough

• • •

Location:
Cache River Natural Area, Vienna
IL/Johnson County

U.S.G.S. Map(s):
1:24,000 Karnak, Vienna

Trail(s) Distance:
two trails total 7.5 miles

Acreage:
1,833 acres

Activities:
hiking, nature study

Fee(s):
none

• • •

19

Heron Pond

Cypress knees

*T*he 9,200 acre Cache River State Natural Area is divided into four separate areas: Heron Pond, Wildcat Bluff, Little Black Slough and Lower Cache River with headquarters located one mile north of Belknap, Illinois. The four separate tracts are miles apart and require separate access points. Land acquisition is under way to expand this natural area. When complete, the Cache River wetlands will cover over 60,000 acres.

*H*eron Pond is a dense bald cypress forest named for the great blue herons which nest and build rookeries in the huge cypress trees, especially in the Little Black Slough Area. The Lower Cache River Area has bald cypress trees over 1,000 years old. They are related to the sequoia and redwood of California's Sierra Mountains and the Pacific Northwest coast and are among the oldest trees east of the Mississippi River. Southern Illinois is at the northern edge of the bald cypress range.

*T*he Heron Pond trailhead begins west of the parking area northeast of Belknap, Illinois. The easy and level path crosses on a wooden suspension bridge over the Upper Cache River and follows the floodplain between the river and Heron Pond. The swamp border and low floodplain forest harbor the Drummond's red maple, red elm, pumpkin ash, overcup oak, pin oak and buttonbush. After a half mile walk into the preserve, a 60 yard-long floating boardwalk invites hikers to explore the center of Heron Pond and a bald cypress forest. Wood ducks and other bird life are common in the swamp forest. Retrace your steps and continue on the forest path. The next half-mile the trail loops uphill through an oak-hickory upland forest that includes tulip, beech, sweet gum, silver maple and other hardwoods. Poison ivy is the main understory plant and is found abundantly along the perimeter of the trail. At this point the trail loops back.

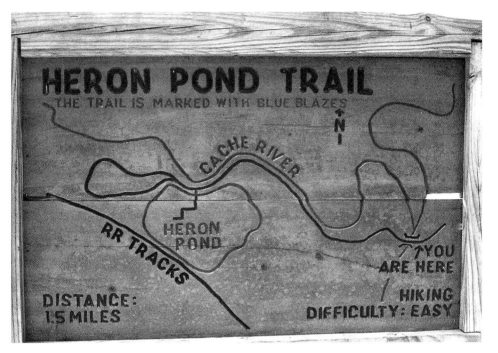

Heron Pond trail sign

Retrace your original steps back to the parking area. Although the trail is obvious, blue blazes at eye level are painted on tree trunks

*T*o reach Heron Pond Nature Preserve from I-24, take exit #16 west at Vienna onto S.R. 146 and drive about two miles to the junction of S.R. 45 in Vienna. Go south on S.R. 45, 4.5 miles and turn left/west on the paved road to Belknap, Illinois. Drive one and one-half miles and turn on the gravel road, approximately one-half mile before the CB&Q railroad tracks. Turn right/north and drive one mile past a farmhouse to the dead-end parking area. Follow the directional signs.

*F*rom I-57, take exit #24 east at Dongola, Illinois and drive about 13 miles to Belknap, Illinois. Continue northeast on the paved road towards S.R. 45 and about one-half mile beyond the CB&Q railroad turn left/north and follow the directional signs to the parking area at the dead end.

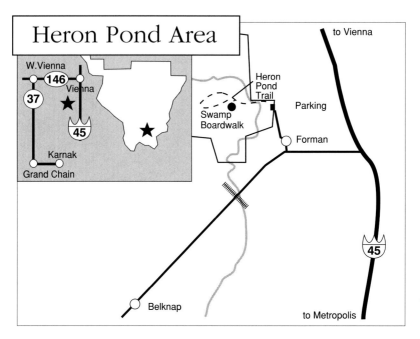

Heron Pond Area

W.Vienna
146
37
Vienna
45
Karnak
Grand Chain

Heron Pond Trail
Parking
Swamp Boardwalk
Forman
to Vienna
45
Belknap
to Metropolis

Heron Pond

• • •

Location:
Cache River Natural Area, Belknap
IL/Johnson County

U.S.G.S. Map(s):
1:24,000 Karnak, Vienna

Trail(s) Distance:
one and one-half miles

Acreage:
1,861 acres

Activities:
hiking, nature study

Fee(s):
none

• • •

Section 8 Woods Nature Preserve

State Champion Tupelo tree

Section 8 Woods Nature Preserve lies along the broad south floodplain of the lower Cache River next to S.R. 37 on the east side of the highway at the Johnson-Pulaski County line, one mile north of the junction with S.R. 169. The preserve is easily accessed by a 500 foot boardwalk that penetrates one of the most outstanding bald cypress and water tupelo swamps in southern Illinois.

Once entering the roadside swamp forest, the visitor is quickly impressed by the enormous old growth trees. Record size tree specimens include overcup oak, water elm, water locust and the Illinois State champion water tupelo that has a measured circumference of nearly 23 feet, a height of 88 feet and a crown spread of 44 feet. Within the Cache River Natural Area there are eight State champions and two national champion trees such as the Drummond red maple, American hornbeam, water hickories, swamp privet, green hawthorn, pumpkin ash, deciduous holly and bald cypress. Several cypress trees along the Cache River set the existing state record. Truly this nature preserve is a "cathedral of woody wetland giants." Retrace your steps back to the parking area. Section 7 across the highway is also a significant swamp lowland forest and riverine natural community.

To reach Section 8 Woods State Nature Preserve from I-57, take exit #18 east near Ullin, Illinois and drive seven miles to S.R. 37. Go north on S.R. 37 two miles and pull off into the roadside parking area on the right/east side of the highway just before the Cache River bridge. The boardwalk, scheduled to be constructed in 1992, begins near the parking area.

As the crow flies two miles east, 1,000 year-old bald cypress trees still thrive on Department of Conservation property and are worth seeing while in the vicinity. From Section 8 Woods Nature Preserve drive one mile south on S.R. 37 to the junction with S.R. 169. Go left/east and drive 2.2 miles and turn left/north. Proceed 1.4 miles across the railroad tracks and the Cache River. The preserve will be on the right/east side of the gravel road. The trees may be easily spotted from the road and the preserve may be entered on foot for closer viewing.

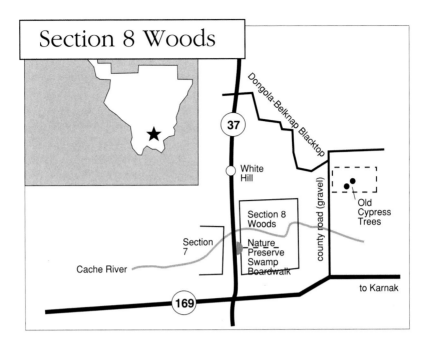

Section 8 Woods

• • •

Location:
Cache River Natural Area, White
Hill, IL/Johnson and Pulaski
Counties

U.S.G.S. Map(s):
1:24,000 Cypress & Karnak

Trail(s) Distance:
500 ft Boardwalk

Acreage:
300 Acres

Activities:
nature walk, handicapped
accessible, nature study

Fee(s):
none

• • •

Limekiln Springs Trail

Interpretive sign at Limekiln Trail

*E*stablished by the Nature Conservancy, Limekiln Springs Trail follows the south floodplain forest border of the Lower Cache River, meandering between wetlands and open meadow. The linear blue blazed path leads from a small parking lot east one mile to culminate at Limekiln Slough and Springs, tributaries of the Cache River. In order to return to the beginning of the trail you must retrace your steps.

*E*nroute numerous plants are identified by common and scientific names including red oak, sugarberry, green ash, American elm, sycamore, giant cane, kingnut hickory, boxelder maple, black walnut, sugar maple, black oak, tulip poplar, spicebush, shagbark hickory, swamp holly, overcup oak, persimmon, pignut hickory, trumpet creeper, sweetgum, paw paw, blue beech, pin oak, cherrybark oak, swamp privet, sassafras, flowering dogwood and bald cypress.

*T*wo wooden bridges cross sloughs halfway through the trail and two interpretive stations have been added to enhance your understanding of the site's natural and social history. For example, visitors learn the high land points were sites of former Indian occupation and early settlers referred to the overflowing Cache River wetlands where the stream and the land were difficult to define, as "Scatters." The area is a critical foraging ground for the rare and endangered gray bats migrating to southern swarming sites.

*T*he place name limekiln is probably connected with the Ullin, Illinois business that thrived in the latter half of the 19th century and into the 20th when large quantities of lime and rock were produced for agriculture and construction. Kiln furnaces were necessary to produce the lime. For more information, a trail brochure guide is available at the trailhead registration box.

*T*he Nature Conservancy cooperates with the U.S. Fish & Wildlife Service, the Illinois Department of Conservation and Ducks Unlimited to protect and restore the Cache River wetlands for prosperity. The joint undertaking will establish over 60,000 acres for the benefit of the wilderness and people.

*T*o reach Limekiln Springs Trail from I-59, take exit #18 near Ullin, Illinois, drive east 2.6 miles to a gravel crossroads and turn left/north. Go one mile north on the gravel road past the Cache Chapel and Cemetery to a parking lot at the right of the closed river bridge.

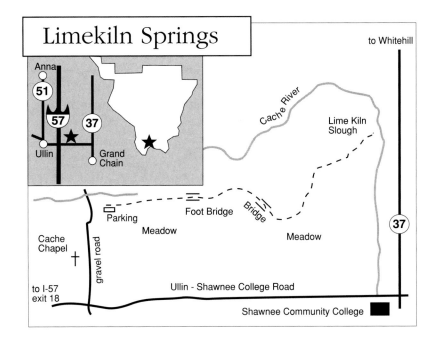

Limekiln Springs Trail

• • •

Location:
Ullin, IL/Pulaski County

U.S.G.S. Map(s):
1:24,000 Cypress

Trail(s) Distance:
one mile one-way (two miles total)

Acreage:
228 Acres

Activities:
hiking, nature study

Fee(s):
none

• • •

Mermet Lake Conservation Area

Informational Sign

*D*esigned for the purpose of attracting waterfowl, Mermet Lake was originally a bald cypress swamp. Surrounded by levees, the 452 acre shallow body of water is seasonally regulated to flood two adjacent walk-in duck hunting areas. Primarily designed for duck hunters, hikers will enjoy the two short, easy loop trails. Bird watchers will discover the lake and sky filled annually with Canada geese, blue and snow geese and other migratory waterfowl. Endangered species such as the purple gallinule, least bittern, swan, and moorhen are occasionally spotted as are osprey and bald eagles. Common cormorants, mergansers, and terns are attracted to the lake and fish for food. Migratory songbirds, especially warblers, usually appear the last week of April and the first week of May. The 26 permanent blinds may also serve birdwatchers who are interested in observing wildlife.

*T*he Mermet Flatwoods Loop Trail is a one mile interpretive trail that begins and ends behind the park office, next to the picnic area near the north entrance. The vehicle-wide forest path penetrates the number one Walk-In Duck Hunting Area which is flooded during the hunting season. Tree identification of wetland species makes the flatwoods level trail more interesting. Be advised, mosquitoes thrive in the poorly drained habitat.

*T*he second trail loops through the 43 acre Mermet Swamp Nature Preserve. The one-half mile self-guiding interpretive trail begins and ends at the extreme southeast area of the lake near the now closed south entrance. An old growth forest of pin oak, swamp white oak and sweet gum thrive at the west end of the preserve. A second growth community of bald cypress, swamp cottonwood and pumpkin ashes are found growing at the swamp. American snowbell, arrow arum, white basswood and red iris are some of the unusual rare plants of the preserve. A short boardwalk extends into and overlooks the cypress swamp. A small parking area accommodates eight to ten vehicles.

*T*o reach Mermet Lake Conservation Area from I-24, take exit #27 west and drive north one and one-half miles to New Columbia, Illinois. Turn left/southwest at the "T" road just beyond New Columbia and proceed five miles to Mermet, Illinois and S.R. 45. Turn left/south and continue one-half mile to Mermet and the Conservation Area next to S.R. 45.

*F*rom I-57, take exit #18 east near Ullin and drive seven miles to S.R. 37. Turn north on S.R. 37, drive one mile, turn east on S.R. 169 and continue on through Karnak and Boaz, Illinois to S.R. 45. Turn south on S.R. 45, proceed one and one-half miles past Mermet, Illinois and drive for another half-mile to the entrance.

*M*ost state sites are open year round except on Christmas Day and New Year's Day.

Moorhen Geese

23

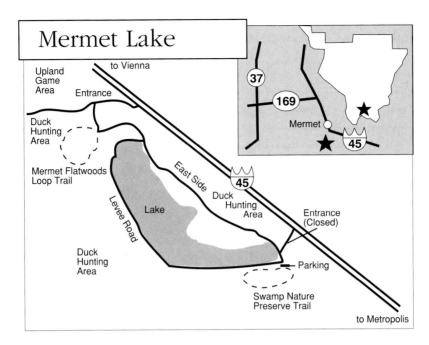

Mermet Lake

Mermet Lake

• • •

Location:
Mermet, IL/Massac County

U.S.G.S. Map(s):
1:24,000 Joppa

Trail(s) Distance:
two trails total one and one-half miles

Acreage:
2,680 acres, 452 acre lake

Activities:
hiking, nature study, picnicking, fishing, 10 hp boating, boat launch ramps, seasonal hunting, nature preserve

Fee(s):
boat rental

• • •

23

Fort Massac State Park

Fort Massac

*O*verlooking the Ohio River, Fort Massac State Park was dedicated in 1908 as the first state park in Illinois, primarily for its historical links. The fortress played a brief but important role in the course of empires during the 18th and 19th century. Spain, France, Great Britain and the United States were involved in the drama of westward expansion and conquest that included Fort Massac. The name Massac is derived from "Massiac," the surname of the French Minister of Colonial Affairs and Marines during the French and Indian War. The French military erected Fort de Massiac in 1757 but it was abandoned following the conclusion of the French and Indian War in 1763. The victorious British discovered the French fort had been burned by Chickasaw Indians and did not rebuild or re-occupy the site, thus leaving their position substantially weakened in Illinois Country. As a result, George Rogers Clark and his "Long Knives" were able during the Revolutionary War to capture, with greater ease for the American cause the British-held Kaskaskia and Fort Sackville at Vincennes

*A*fter the Revolutionary War, Fort Massac was rebuilt by orders from President Washington. It was destroyed by the powerful and devastating New Madrid Earthquake in 1811-1812 but was soon rebuilt as a fortification during the War of 1812 only to be forgotten until the Civil War. A measles epidemic in 1861-1862 claimed many lives and the Union forces abandoned Fort Massac for the last time. Notable historic personalities associated with Fort Massac include Commander MaCarty, St. Ange de Bell Rive, Father Mermet, Zebulon Montgomery Pike, Lewis and Clark, Captain Daniel Bissell, General James Wilkinson, Tecumseh, Pontiac, Andrew Jackson and Aaron Burr. Author Everett Hale's American historical novel, "The Man Without

Morel mushrooms

A Country," takes place at Fort Massac where Aaron Burr and General Wilkinson plot treason against the United States and draw up plans to conquer the American Southwest and Mexico.

*T*he American timber fort of 1794 has been reconstructed and is open to the public for visitation and tours. A historic museum features displays of artifacts found from the site revealing the fort's characteristics and the soldier's daily life. A statue of George Rogers Clark overlooks the Ohio River. Living history weekends and the annual Fort Massac encampment recreate life during the early years when nations struggled for possession of the New World.

*P*ark visitors will discover the surrounding natural areas of Fort Massac along two easy trails, east of the fort. The Long Knife Trail is a one and one-half mile loop that begins and ends at the Long Knife picnic area across from the fort parking lot and park office. The level and well-used trail encircles a floodplain forest and the Cherokee Point picnic area. Further east is the two and one-half mile Hickory Nut Trail that is a half loop or full loop trail if you follow the paved park road. This Ohio River woodland bluff trail makes a fine year-round hike with excellent views of the mile wide stream. Osprey, herons, hawks, ring-billed gulls and shorebirds may be spotted.

I nterstate 24 divides the park into west and east sections. East and north of I-24 is the 244 acre Massac Forest Nature Preserve. The forest area includes bald cypress swamps, pin and swamp white oak flatwoods, floodplain forests of cottonwood, pecan, American elm, black willow, sweet gum and cherrybark oak as well as upland forest with many wildflowers. State endangered plants include storax, water elm and mock bishop's weed. There are no trails in the preserve but visitors are free to wander.

To reach Fort Massac State Park from I-24, take exit #37 west onto U.S. 45 towards Metropolis, Illinois. The park entrance is about two and one-half miles west of the interstate exchange. The park is open daily year around from 7:00 a.m. to 10:00 p.m. The Historic Museum is open daily from 10:00 a.m. to 5:30 p.m. Guided tours are available by pre-arrangement with the site superintendent. Most state properties are open year around except on Christmas Day and New Year's Day.

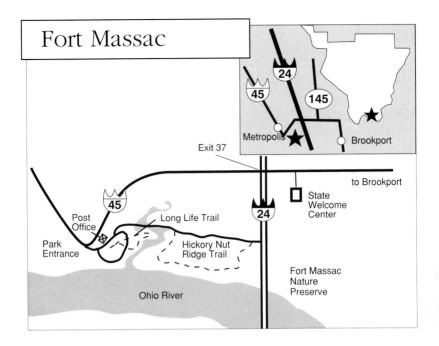

Fort Massac

Exit 37

Metropolis

Brookport

to Brookport

State
Welcome
Center

Post
Office

Long Life Trail

Park
Entrance

Hickory Nut
Ridge Trail

Fort Massac
Nature
Preserve

Ohio River

Fort Massac State Park

• • •

Location:
Metropolis, IL/Massac County

U.S.G.S. Map(s):
1:24,000 Metropolis, IL-KY

Trail(s) Distance:
two trails total four miles

Acreage:
1,470 acres

Activities:
hiking, nature study, historic site, museum,
nature preserve, picnicking, shelters,
playgrounds, river fishing, boating, boat ramp,
seasonal hunting, camping, special events

Fee(s):
camping

• • •

24

Lake of Egypt Recreation Area

Lake of Egypt

*L*ake of Egypt is a privately owned 2,300 acre man made lake that was constructed in 1963 to furnish water to cool the steam generating plant at the dam site owned and operated by Southern Illinois Power Co-operative. A good portion of the 93 miles of finger cove shoreline has been developed as residential subdivisions. Privately owned public recreational marinas are located at Pyramid Acres including Lake of Egypt marina on Egyptian Hills. The Shawnee National Forest Service maintains 1,600 acres of shoreline on the southeast side. Unfortunately, developed trails have not been established, but the old and new roads, fishermen's paths and off road rambling provide foot access. Undesignated user paths skirt the lakeshore at the picnic, boat ramp and campground areas. Forest roads 870A, 870B and 873 are not far from the campground and may be hiked. Trail development is in the planning stage. The lake is known for its fine fishing of largemouth bass, striped bass, bluegill and crappie.

*L*ake of Egypt Recreation Area is located seven miles south of Marion, Illinois and three miles east of I-57. The National Forest site is located about seven miles south and west of Creal Springs on gravel road 1725 north and F.R. 870.

*T*o reach Lake of Egypt Recreation Area from I-57, take exit #45 east on S.R. 148 onto S.R 37. Go south on S.R. 37 to Goreville, Illinois and continue south of town. Go east on 1075E Tunnel Hill blacktop and follow the directional signs turning north on 1725N Creal Springs Road and west on F.R. 870. From I-24, exit 7 east on 1075E Tunnel Hill Road and then northwest on Creal Springs Road 1725N and F.R. 870. The road is paved but turns to gravel for the last few miles. The campground is two miles west of Creal Springs Road.

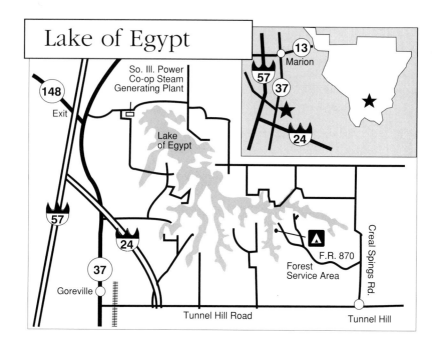

Lake of Egypt Recreation Area

• • •

Location:
Shawnee National Forest, Goreville
IL/Johnson & Williamson Counties

U.S.G.S. Map(s):
1:24,000 Creal Springs, Goreville

Trail(s) Distance:
no established trails

Acreage:
1,600 acres land, 2,300 acre lake

Activities:
nature study, picnicking, shelters,
boat launch, boating, fishing, water
skiing, camping

Fee(s):
camping, boat permit daily

• • •

Dutchman Lake

Blufftop Waterfall at Dutchman Lake

*C*onstructed and impounded in the early 1970's, 118 acre Dutchman Lake is popular with people who fish. Until recently, the forest service maintained the Dutchman Lake Trail, a two mile loop that followed the northeast shoreline and sandstone blufftops. The adventuresome may enjoy locating and hiking the abandoned and overgrown unmarked trail, especially in late fall, winter and early spring months when the leaves are down.

*T*he former trailhead segments leading from the boat ramp, pit toilet and pull off parking area to the first stream, a distance of about 100 yards, is obscure, but beyond that the old trail is still obvious. Walking northwest another 300 yards the old trail crosses a finger cove and stream inlet. The trail leads up to the bluff and heads east along the red cedar tree-lined cliff. Vistas of Dutchman Lake are excellent. The lake and its tributaries form the headwaters of Dutchman Creek that flow south to join with the Cache River. Seasonal waterfalls cascade to the hillside below. Horse riders occasionally use the trail and their limited impact helps to keep the trail from becoming overgrown. The trail ends at the main entrance road, uphill several hundred yards from the boat ramp and parking pull out. Hopefully in the future the trail will be restored. Plans are being made for the River-to-River Trail to pass through the area.

*T*o reach Dutchman Lake from I-24, take exit #14 onto U.S. 45 and drive south 0.7 miles to the first country road on the right/west side of the highway about one and one-half miles north of Vienna, Illinois. Turn right and go 60 yards to a "T" then turn right/north on C.R. 1000N. Proceed three miles on C.R. 1000N to the main entry road of Dutchman Lake and turn left/west. Drive one mile to the boat ramp, pit toilet and roadside parking pull out. Follow the directional signs.

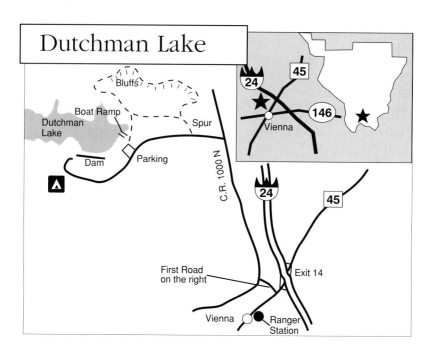

Dutchman Lake

• • •

Location:
Shawnee National Forest, Goreville
IL/Johnson County

U.S.G.S. Map(s):
1:24,000 Bloomfield, Vienna

Trail(s) Distance:
no maintained trails

Activities:
hiking, nature study, fishing,
boating, boat ramp, primitive
camping

Fee(s):
none

• • •

Ferne Clyffe State Park

Trail sign at Ferne Clyffe Lake

*F*erne Clyffe has long been considered a special area because of the Late Woodland artifacts discovered there. These findings indicate that the rock overhangs were used for shelter as long ago as 500 B.C. In 1778 the Revolutionary War hero George Rogers Clark and his Kentucky "Long Knives" passed through the land enroute to seize Kaskaskia from the British. The Cherokee were in the area from 1838-1839 as they moved across southern Illinois in route to the West.

*I*n more recent times, the Dennison brothers of Cairo, Illinois in 1899 purchased the rocky hollow that contains the park's largest shelter bluff, named Hawk's Cave. A few years later Emma Rebman, a school teacher, acquired the 150 acre property and is believed to have named the park Ferne Clyffe for the abundance and variety of ferns. The Old English spelling is of uncertain origin but the name is believed to be derived from Miss Rebman's romantic nature. She began charging a small admission fee to her preserve of canyons, dells, brooks and cascades in the 1920s when her property was considered by authorities to be "the most beautiful spot in Illinois." Thanks to her untiring efforts as a conservationist, the land was deeded to the State of Illinois in 1949.

*N*ature walkers will appreciate the short and long trails of Ferne Clyffe State Park. The ten easy to difficult, maintained pathways lead visitors to bluffs, rock shelters, rock formations, canyons, waterfalls, brooks, meadows, hollows and Ferne Clyffe Lake. Trails #1 to #6 interconnect, Trail #8 encircles a nature preserve and Trails #7, #9 and #10 traverse Happy Hollow in the west area of the park.

*T*he Rebman Trail or Trail #1 is a quarter-mile easy, level, loop trail that leads through boulder breakdown to a waterfall in Little Rocky Hollow.

Waterfall at trail terminus at Big Rocky Hollow Trail

A memorial plaque honoring Emma Rebman is situated at the trailhead. Her favorite quotation is featured:

To him who, in the love of nature holds communion with her
visible forms, she speaks a various language for his gayer hours.

Adjacent west of the Rebman Trail is the one mile loop Trail #2 or Hawk's Cave Trail. It is not considered a true cave but rather a shelter cave. The huge protruding ledge of eroded rock makes an high arching roof that measures 150 feet-long. The forested shady path leading to Hawk's Cave is considered easy.

Nearby is Trail #3 or the Big Rocky Hollow Trail that begins at the cul-de-sac turn-around next to the parking lot near Hillside picnic shelter. The linear trail is a one mile level hike round trip alongside a scenic brook that leads upstream to a 100 foot waterfall at the end of a box canyon. A variety of ferns thrive in the cool, moist and shaded canyon, particularly on the Pennsylvanian sandstone boulders.

You may also access Trail #4 or the Waterfall Trail connecting the upper bluffs and Deer Ridge campground from Trail #3. This three-quarter mile spur trail is actually designed for campers to reach the waterfall and the lower hollow Trails #1, #2 and #3.

Trail #5 or the Blackjack Oak Trail begins or ends next to the Hillside picnic shelter and leads uphill to run along Deer Ridge. The red cedar and blackjack oak blufftop trail extends for one mile and descends to Ferne Clyffe Lake and Trail #6. The gnarled and scrubby oak tree with its three lobed leaves prefers the dry exposed cliffs of the Shawnee Hills. Open vistas to the west and Happy Hollow have been established and benches provided. Campers may access the trail from spurs in Deer Ridge campground.

Shelter overhang at Ferne Clyffe

*T*rail #6 or the Ferne Clyffe Lake Trail is a one mile shoreline trail that encircles the 16 acre man-made lake. The trailhead has a parking area and across the park road is the south terminus of the Blackjack Oak Trail. The lakeside trail is popular with fishermen.

*L*ocated just southwest of Ferne Clyffe Lake is Trail #8 or the Round Bluff Nature Preserve Trail that begins and ends at the Lakeview picnic shelter parking area. Several of the plants found here occur nowhere else in southern Illinois and are actually more common in wet acid soils of the northeastern United States and Canada. The north and northeast facing bluffs support the rare hay-scented fern, cinnamon fern, black chokeberry, bartonia

27

gentian, closed gentian and fameflower. The drier and warmer southern bluffs support prickly pear cactus, small flowered rock pink and blue curls. The one mile moderate loop guides hikers around the base of the honeycombed rock bluff.

*T*rail #9 or the Happy Hollow Backpack Trail leads backpackers from the primitive camping parking area downhill to Trail #7 and Trail #10. At the trail junction, Trail #9 goes left/south a short way to a spur trail and the backpack canyon area. Trail #9 is one-half miles one way. Backpack campers are encouraged to call the park office (618-995-2411) in advance of their visit.

*T*rail #7 or the Happy Hollow Trail also begins and ends at the primitive camping/parking area and the Bluff Views picnic area. The 5.5 mile trail joins with Trail #10, the Happy Hollow Horse Trail, as it forms a long narrow loop through forest and revegetating fields.

*T*rail #10 or the Happy Hollow Horse Trail begins and ends at the horse camping area and is eight miles. Open to hikers, the horse trail continues north to the park boundary and Goreville, Illinois.

*T*he state park is easily accessed from I-57 and I-24. To reach Ferne Clyffe from I-57, take exit #40 east at C.R. 13 and drive 3.5 miles to Goreville, Illinois and the junction of S.R. 37. Go south on S.R. 37, one and one-half miles to the park entrance. From I-24, take exit #7 west and drive three miles to S.R. 37 and turn left/south and drive one-half mile to the park entrance. Ferne Clyffe is open year around.

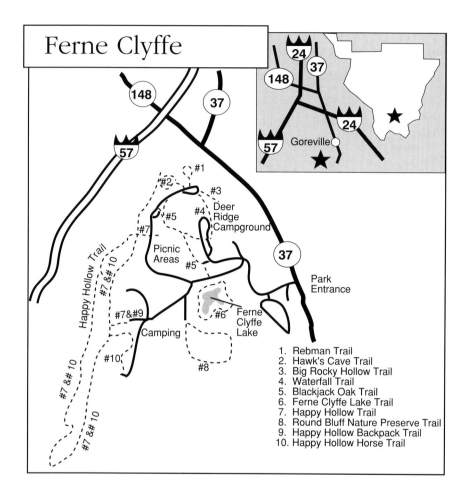

Ferne Clyffe

24

37

148

Goreville

57

24

148

37

57

Deer
Ridge
Campground

Picnic
Areas

Happy Hollow Trail

37

Park
Entrance

#1

#2

#3

#4

#5

#5

#5

#7

#7 & #10

#7 & #9

#6

Ferne
Clyffe
Lake

Camping

#10

#8

#7 & #10

#7 & #10

1. Rebman Trail
2. Hawk's Cave Trail
3. Big Rocky Hollow Trail
4. Waterfall Trail
5. Blackjack Oak Trail
6. Ferne Clyffe Lake Trail
7. Happy Hollow Trail
8. Round Bluff Nature Preserve Trail
9. Happy Hollow Backpack Trail
10. Happy Hollow Horse Trail

Ferne Clyffe State Park

• • •

Location:
Goreville, IL/Johnson County

U.S.G.S. Map(s):
1:24,000 Goreville

Trail(s) Distance:
ten trails total 20 miles

Acreage:
1,100 acres

Activities:
hiking, nature study, nature preserve, picnicking, shelters, playgrounds, fishing, hunting, bridle trails, class A & D camping, youth group, horse and backpack, campgrounds

Fee(s):
shelter reservations, camping

• • •

Murphysboro District

Crab Orchard National Wildlife Refuge

Rocky Bluff Trail along Grassy Creek

*O*ne of over 400 National Wildlife Refuges in the United States, Crab Orchard National Wildlife Refuge is a vast area consisting of nearly 9,000 acres of lake water alone. The refuge also encompasses natural and wilderness areas, wildlife food plots and farm pasture on the remaining 34,000 acres. The United States Fish and Wildlife Service and the Department of the Interior administer this significant wildlife sanctuary.

*C*rab Orchard, Little Grassy and Devils Kitchen Lakes are the winter home for 120,000 Canada Geese. This is one of the largest populations in the United States. Bald eagles also come south in the winter to feed from the ice-free lakes. A bird list is available from the refuge headquarters that identifies 245 bird species that visit the Mississippi Flyway man-made stopover. Closed areas off limits to the public are posted with blue and white signs. Unfortunately the scenic spillway waterfall area is closed to public visitation.

*O*ne of the few maintained trails is located north of the refuge headquarters on the northeast side of 6,965 acre Crab Orchard Lake. The one-mile self-guiding loop Chamnesstown School Trail has 14 interpretive stops that describe forest ecology, migratory waterfowl and wildlife management practices. If you decide not to hike the entire earth path loop there is a shorter half-mile loop that runs down the center of the woods and pine plantation. The trailhead begins next to the parking area, west and next to the log house Chamnesstown School north of A-3 Road. In addition, several miles of auto tour route begin at the Chamnesstown School and Trail parking area and follow A-3 Road, Wolf Creek Road and A-5 Road west and north. A second maintained nature trail is located at the north shore Crab Orchard campground and is designed primarily for campers. The trail

Canada Geese eggs

follows the shoreline of the peninsular-shaped point. This is a daily fee area.

*F*ire lanes are hikeable and the best in the Crab Orchard Lake area are along the southwest shore north of Spillway Road between Dogwood Lane Observation Area and Grassy Bay. The linear, non-looping fire lanes follow the high ground of finger points that extend into Crab Orchard Lake.

A few miles south of Crab Orchard Lake and east of Giant City State Park are the wooded shores of the "Sister Lakes": Devils Kitchen and Little Grassy. Both man-made lakes border the wilderness areas to the south. The wilderness area is home to a diverse flora and fauna and is open to the hiker and hunter. Wilderness Trail Road 17 on the southeast shore finger cove of Devils Kitchen is hikeable and is considered handicapped accessible. The one and one-half mile easy loop is an abandoned paved road that borders the wilderness area and the lake. Park before the loop road 17 bridge crossing in the spacious parking area just west of the bridge. This trail is easily accessed from Grassy Road or Wolf Creek Road. A second loop trail follows an old service road in the southwest wilderness area of Devils Kitchen Lake. The two mile foot trail loop skirts a headwater finger cove beneath a maturing forest cover. Trailhead parking is located south of loop road #9 accessible from Rocky Comfort Road through Grassy Road.

*T*he north end of the 810 acre lake near the dam features camping, picnicking, fishing, and boat ramps. Shoreline loop roads numbered 1 to 17 surround Devils Kitchen Lake. Two interconnecting hiking trails have been established on the northeast side of Devils Kitchen Lake southeast of the campground alongside Devils Kitchen Road.

*T*he one and one-quarter mile Rocky Bluff Trail begins just south of the Grassy Creek bridge at a parking pullout across from Line Road #11, 0.7 miles south of the campground. The forest path follows the stream where sandstone rock outcrops and waterfalls are numerous. Interpretive trail signs are posted for a greater understanding of the general ecology of the area. The trail heads uphill to connect the Wild Turkey Trail. Go right/west a few yards to reconnect the Rocky Bluff Trail and walk downhill to form a complete loop at Grassy Creek or you may walk the linear fire lane path of Wild Turkey Trail that extends from Devils Kitchen Lake Road across from Line Road #12 east to a metal gate at Grassy Road. The distance both ways is three miles through pine plantations and hardwood forests. Wild Turkey Trail access is 1.6 miles south of the campground.

*L*ittle Grassy Lake is situated about two miles directly west of Devils Kitchen Lake and borders Giant City State Park and Southern Illinois University's Touch of Nature. Private group camps are established on the east and northwest lake shore. The northwest shore is where the public marina, boat ramp, and campground are located. Little Grassy Lake occupies 1,000 water acres and has 30 miles of shoreline. Hiking is limited.

*T*he 4,050 acre wilderness area of the refuge is located to the immediate south of Little Grassy Lake and Devils Kitchen Lake. The fire lanes or service roads are hikeable however access is limited and camping is not permitted in the wilderness area. Panther Den Wilderness of the Shawnee National Forest adjoins the Crab Orchard National Wildlife Refuge south of Devils Kitchen Lake. Hopefully, these areas will be hikeable in the near future.

You may want to visit the 115 acre Little Grassy State Fish Hatchery located next to the Crab Orchard National Wildlife Refuge just north of Little Grassy Lake via Grassy Road/C.R. 24. Fish produced at the hatchery are used for stocking water bodies statewide. The modern warm-water fish hatchery may be viewed from the observation area and tours are on a self-guided basis. Visitors' hours are daily from 8:00 a.m. to 3:30 p.m. Employee guided tours can be scheduled for large groups. A three-quarter mile linear hiking trail begins at the fish hatchery building parking area and follows alongside the main paved access road to end and begin near the entrance.

Crab Orchard Lake runs parallel to S.R. 13, four miles east of Carbondale and three miles south and east of Carterville, Illinois. To reach Crab Orchard National Wildlife Refuge from I-5, take exit #54A-B west at Marion, Illinois onto S.R. 13 and continue towards Carbondale, Illinois. To reach Chamnesstown School Trail and the refuge headquarters, exit S.R. 148 two mile south of the junction of S.R. 13. There are several access roads from S.R. 13 along the north shore of Crab Orchard Lake where most of the facilities of this lake are found.

To reach Devils Kitchen and Little Grassy Lakes from I-57, take exit #45 northwest onto S.R. 148 to Grassy Road and adjoining accesses.

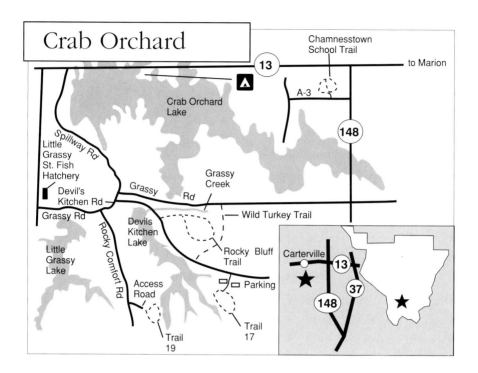

Crab Orchard

Chamnesstown
School Trail

to Marion

13

A-3

Crab Orchard
Lake

148

Spillway Rd

Little
Grassy
St. Fish
Hatchery

Grassy
Creek

Devil's
Kitchen Rd

Grassy Rd

Grassy Rd

Wild Turkey Trail

Devils
Kitchen
Lake

Little
Grassy
Lake

Rocky Comfort Rd

Rocky Bluff
Trail

Carterville

13

Access
Road

Parking

37

148

Trail
17

Trail
19

28

• • •

Location:
Carterville, IL/Williamson County

U.S.G.S. Map(s):
1:24,000 Crab Orchard Lake,
Carbondale, Lick Creek

Trail(s) Distance:
five trails total 8.4 miles

Acreage:
43,000 land & water acres

Activities:
hiking, nature study, picnicking,
shelters, bicycling, fishing, beach
swimming, wind surfing, boating,
boat launch ramps, marinas, docks,
boat rentals, campgrounds,
concessions

Fee(s):
boat rentals, beach use, camping

• • •

Trail 29

Carbondale Nature Places

Geodesic picnic shelter dome at Campus Lake

*T*he City of Carbondale, the home of Southern Illinois University, is the cultural and educational center of Southern Illinois. The community has fine public parks, administered by the Carbondale Park District, providing active recreation in passive natural surroundings. The District's headquarters are located on the northwest side of a five acre site known as Hickory Lodge at 1115 West Sycamore Street. The beautifully landscaped grounds and formal gardens of Hickory Lodge have served as the site for numerous outdoor weddings. Also located on the northwest side at 940 North Oakland, is the five acre Oakdale Park known for its mature stand of oak and hickory trees providing an outdoor haven for many of God's little creatures.

*O*n the town's northeast side is the 28 acre Attucks Park. Located at 400 to 800 North Wall Street, it features walking trails, natural areas, picnicking facilities, playgrounds and multi-use sports play fields.

*L*ocated on the community's southeast side are four sites known as Tatum Heights Park, the Greenway/Bikeway, Doug Lee Park and the William Marberry Arboretum. The eight acre Tatum Heights Park located at Cedarview and Cindy Streets, features natural areas, picnicking facilities, playgrounds and multi use sports play fields. The ten acre Greenway and Bikeway includes a three-fourth mile hard surface path following the west bank of Pyles Fork Creek from East Grand Avenue to East Walnut Street. The Greenway and Bikeway also provides eight acres of natural habitat. The nine acre Doug Lee Park located at 1200 East Grand Avenue consists of four outdoor multi-use sports fields and numerous flowering trees and flower beds. Located on the far southeast side at the intersection of Pleasant Hill Road and South Wall Street is the 25 acre William Marberry Arboretum. The arboretum includes more than 600 different species and varieties of exotic plants, including more than 2,000 dogwood trees and 40 varieties of American holly.

*O*n the city's southwest side is Evergreen Park, Lenus Turley Park, Parrish Park and LIFE Community Center. The 150 acre Evergreen Park located south of Reservoir Road, one-half mile west of U.S. 51, features numerous natural areas, picnicking facilities, playgrounds, multi-use sports fields and fishing. The 4.3 acre Lenus Turley Park, located at the intersection of Illinois Route 13 and North Glenview, features sheltered picnicking, playgrounds, meandering walkways, formal rose gardens and is the site for the summer Sunset Concert series. The 52 acres of Parish Park North and South and the LIFE Community Center are located at 2500 West Sunset. The parks feature nine soccer fields with several acres of natural habitat along the west bank of Little Crab Orchard Creek. The LIFE Community Center features an indoor pool operated year-round and is the home of the District's Alice Wright Day Care providing Illinois licensed child care for children ages three through five.

*L*ocated just beyond the far northwest side of the community is the recently acquired 256 acre site to serve as the home of the District's proposed public golf center. The golf center design proposes the development of 18 holes of regulation golf, nine holes of executive golf, a wee links, a miniature golf facility and a driving range. The opening of the 18 hole golf course, driving range and miniature golf course is scheduled for the summer of 1993. Other amenities proposed include a walking and jogging trail around the perimeter of the golf center site and a ten acre lake.

*N*ear the south center of Carbondale is Southern Illinois University campus which is beautiful to walk about year-round. In the middle of campus is a mature black oak forest called Thompson Woods which is nice to walk through on the shaded paths. The woods are named in honor of a former Civil War veteran who left his property to the university on the condition that the grove be preserved. South of Thompson Woods along Douglas Drive is the campus beach and boat docks on the Campus Lake. A short paved trail leads around the wooded lakeshore where geodesic dome picnic shelters have been provided.

*T*he university's museum features displays of anthropology, archaeology, geology, social and natural history of southern Illinois. The facilities of the museum include a lecture auditorium, sculpture garden and gift shop. The admission, guided tours and programs are free of charge and accessible to all. The hours are 9:00 a.m. to 3:00 p.m. Monday through Friday and 1:30 p.m. to 4:30 p.m. on Sunday when classes are in session. The museum is located in Faner Hall, C-Wing on the University of Southern Illinois University campus.

*T*hree additional Carbondale preserves, established by Green Earth, Inc., are located in the suburban areas. Green Earth Inc. is a private non-profit corporation that organized to procure, manage and maintain lands suitable for the establishment of a system of natural areas for the people of Carbondale. Using proceeds from grants, membership dues and donations, Green Earth Inc. has purchased three parcels known as Green Earth I Woodland Preserve, Green Earth II Prairie Preserve and Green Earth III Wetlands Preserve totaling 47.5 acres. The woodland and prairie tracts are developed with trails and trail guides. Pamphlets are available at the trailheads. Green Earth, Inc.

also sponsors educational field trips to the properties in conjunction with school and community groups.

*G*reen Earth I Woodland Preserve consists of 23 acres of forest and successional field on Brush Hill at the southeast side of Carbondale off Lewis Lane next to a fire station. The one-half mile interpretive trail is dedicated to the memory of Herbie Beyler, one of the founders of Green Earth. The easy to moderate dirt path features 17 stations that correspond to a trail brochure. Three distinct plant communities are located in the preserve: steep upland oak-hickory, lowland beech-maple and regrowth in an old field.

*G*reen Earth II Prairie Preserve is located on the north side of Carbondale adjacent and east of Oakland Avenue Cemetery and lying parallel to the old Illinois Central Railroad right-of-way to Murphysboro, Illinois and Owen Street. The 7.5 acre level tract of prairie and young woodland is accessible by a quarter mile foot path. The small prairie features bluestems, Indian grass, switchgrass, sideoats grama, ratttlesnake master, prairie dock and black-eyed Susan. Before settlement, two-thirds of Illinois was covered with prairie and today only 1,300 acres or two square miles exist. Bluebird boxes have been placed to encourage these scarce cheerful songsters to home here. The low lying woodland portion has several wildflowers, maples, oak, hickory, walnut and persimmon. It is frequently flooded during heavy rains. After your walk you may want to picnic in the nearby wooded grove Oakdale Park, a Carbondale city park located two blocks south at 940 North Oakland.

*T*he Green Earth III Wetland Preserve was the third tract acquired by Green Earth, Inc. The 17 acre tract is located in the southwest corner of the city adjoining Chautauqua Street, lying west of Emerald Lane and east of Little Crab Orchard Creek. The property accesses

Chautauqua Street on the South and Freeman Street on the East. Steps have been taken to restore the old pasture to a wetland prairie site. Future plans for the woodland area at the north end of the tract include nature trails.

*C*arbondale, Illinois is located 15 miles west of I-57 at Marion, Illinois. Exit #54A-B onto S.R. 13 and proceed west.

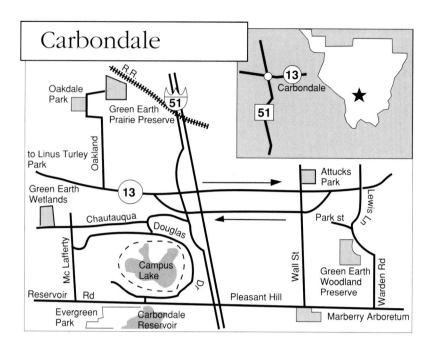

Carbondale

Oakdale Park

R.R.

Green Earth Prairie Preserve

51

13 Carbondale

51

to Linus Turley Park

Oakland

Green Earth Wetlands

13

Attucks Park

Lewis Ln

Chautauqua

Douglas

Park st

Mc Lafferty

Campus Lake

Wall St

Green Earth Woodland Preserve

Warden Rd

Reservoir Rd

Dr

Pleasant Hill

Evergreen Park

Carbondale Reservoir

Marberry Arboretum

29

Carbondale Nature Places

• • •

Location:
Carbondale, IL/Jackson County

Activities:
parks, preserves, museums,
arboretum

Fee(s):
none

• • •

Touch of Nature Environmental Center

Touch of Nature sign

*T*ouch of Nature Environmental Center is a facility owned and maintained by Southern Illinois University. The university facility provides training opportunities for university students and sponsors conferences, programs and workshops for teachers and special populations. The "living and learning" center is nationally outstanding in the fields of therapeutic and outdoor recreation and experiential education. Environmental and interpretive fee-charge programs and workshops are offered to the public on weekends during the school year. Three loop nature trails and a canoe trail are open to the public during the daylight hours year-round.

*T*he Woodland World Trail features 20 stations that identifies trees and forest ecology concepts in a young woods and revegetating meadow. The earth path begins and ends adjacent to the nature center and small pond. The Secondary Succession Trail requires about 30-45 minutes of walking through newly-abandoned fields to end at a climax forest on the west shore of Little Grassy Lake. There are 12 stations; one that includes a quadrant study. The trail begins and ends two tenths of a mile south of the nature center along the road next to a farm house. The 35 station Sunshine Trail describes and applies such ecological terms as food web and chain, succession and environment. The trail begins on an old lane just south of the parking area at Camp II and leads through a maturing deciduous forest ravine, slope and edge, skirting Little Grassy Lake and ending at the south side of the dining hall. Trail brochures and other information is available at the administration house near the entrance.

*T*ouch of Nature borders on the west shore of Little Grassy Lake of Crab Orchard National Wildlife Refuge. Anyone is welcome to canoe the 1,000 acre lake and follow the one mile linear

Little Grassy Lake

shoreline Little Grassy Lake Canoe Trail. The canoe trail begins at the Camp II boat dock area and ends at a point one mile north of the docks. The canoe trail requires 45 minutes to one hour one way. Fifteen interpretive stations have been established along the shore and an excellent trail brochure is available at the main office.

To reach Touch of Nature Environmental Center from 1-57, take exit #54A-B west at Marion onto S.R. 13 and drive about 13 miles. Just before the shopping mall watch for signs indicating Little Grassy Lake and Touch of Nature. Turn left/south onto Giant City Road and drive eight miles to the Touch of Nature entrance on the left/east side of the road. The facility's hours are Monday through Friday are 8:00 a.m. to 4:30 p.m. Please stop by the administrative office to inform staff of your visit and obtain information.

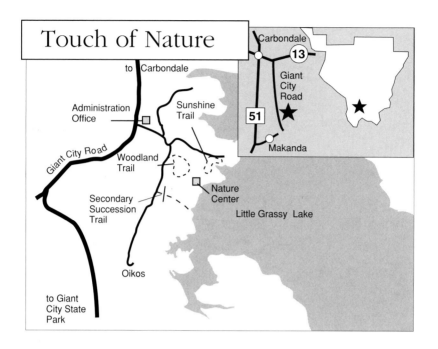

Touch of Nature Environmental Center

• • •

Location:
Carbondale, IL/Jackson &
Williamson Counties

U.S.G.S. Map(s):
1:24,000 Carbondale, Makanda

Trail(s) Distance:
three trails, 2.25 miles

Acreage:
3,100 acres

Activities:
nature trails, nature study,
canoeing, environmental
education center, seasonal
programs

Fee(s):
seasonal programs

• • •

Giant City State Park

Devil's Standtable

*L*ong known for its beautiful rock formations and hardwood forests, Giant City State Park is one of the most popular attractions in southern Illinois. The name, "Giant City" was derived from a group of huge sandstone blocks that separated from a parent ledge to form "avenues" or "streets" that are accessible on foot and are best viewed along Giant City Trail. Besides several short and long trails, the rustic state park offers a rich variety of outdoor recreational pursuits.

*T*he most popular hike is the Giant City Nature Trail, a one mile semi-rugged loop that encircles a bluff where the "city" of giant Makanda sandstone blocks and rock formations may be explored. A self-guiding interpretive brochure is available from the park office. The well-used trail is located off the main park road at picnic area #3 between the lodge and Devil's Standtable Nature Trail.

*T*he Devil's Standtable is a joint mushroom-shaped rock. Many of the locals thought the formation looked like a pulpit for "Old Scratch." A one-third mile loop encircles the rock formation to return to the main park road, picnic and parking area just south of the park office. There is also a shelter cave above the creek.

*U*pridge and adjacent to the Devil's Standtable Trail is the Post Oak Trail, a one-third mile paved path that loops about a small pond via foot bridges. The trail is accessible to the handicapped and equipped with braille readings for the blind. The trailhead and parking is along the upper main park road loop. A trail brochure is available between the softball diamond and park office where the old interpretive center log cabin is located.

*I*ndian Creek Shelter and Nature Trail is found northeast of the Post Oak Trail and softball diamond along the park road to the group campground. The three-fourths mile semi-rugged loop

Trilliums along Trillium Trail

31

trail leads to virgin forest and rock shelter bluffs that were occupied by the Late Woodland Period Indians from 400 A.D. to 1100 A.D. A trail brochure is available to inform the hiker and to enhance the walk.

*N*orth of the park office near the north main entrance is the Stone Fort Nature Trail and Fern Rock Nature Preserve. Stone Fort like Indian Creek Shelter was occupied by the Late Woodland people about 600 A.D. to 800 A.D. The 80 foot high sandstone bluff is accessible on foot along a mile-long moderate trail. At the east end where the bluff connects with the larger ridge, the former inhabitants erected a stone wall, carrying the rock from the stream bed below to completely enclose the bluff or isolate it. The tower-like bluff was believed to have been used for defensive purposes.

*A*cross the park road from Stone Fort is the 110 acre Fern Rock Nature Preserve where shooting stars, rare mints and trilliums thrive undisturbed. The two mile rugged Trillium Trail loop begins and ends near the Makanda, Illinois entrance to Giant City State Park. The trail follows the base of the 100 foot bluff where many spring wildflowers may be enjoyed. Near Stone Fort across the road the trail goes uphill to the blufftop and loops back along the edge, eventually to descend back to the original trailhead. There are several caves and rock shelters along the route. A trail brochure is available.

*T*he longest and most rugged hike in Giant City State Park is the 16 mile Red Cedar Trail Loop. Parking is available at the trailhead at the southwest end of the tent campground next to the family campground. Overnight backpackers will need a fee permit to camp in the backcountry Red Cedar Camp. The trail is blazed with white and orange circles that appear at eye-level on trees. It required two years to build the trail through such places as Indian Creek, pine plantations, Old Makanda and pioneer coal mines. The Red Cedar Trail is near the park perimeter most of the time. Carry your necessary water. A trail brochure is available. Additional points of interest include the climbable 82 foot spiral water tower with a 52 foot high observation deck. The tower is located at Giant City Lodge, a magnificent massive rock and wood lodge built by the Civilian Conservation Corps in 1939 and where fried chicken is the speciality.

*T*o reach Giant City State Park from I-57, take exit #30 west onto S.R. 146 to Anna, Illinois or 54A-B onto S.R. 13 west to Carbondale, Illinois and the junction with S.R. 51. From Anna go north 15 miles and from Carbondale go south 12 miles on S.R. 51 to Makanda, Illinois then east to Giant City State Park's north main entrance.

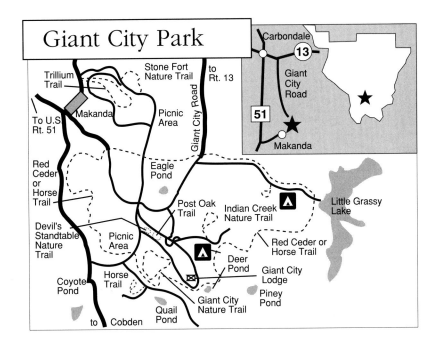

Giant City State Park

• • •

Location:
Makanda, IL/Jackson Union
Counties

U.S.G.S. Map(s):
1:24,000 Makanda, Carbondale

Trail(s) Distance:
seven trails total 18.5 miles

Activities:
hiking, nature study, picnicking,
shelters, playgrounds, lake fishing,
boating (ten mph. limit), boat launch
ramp, bridle trails, riding, stable,
seasonal hunting, rappelling, nature
preserve, archeological site, backpacking,
class A, C & D horse campgrounds,
lodge, concessions

Fee(s):
camping, boat, horse rentals

• • •

31

Lake Murphysboro State Park

Lake Murphysboro

*T*he seven and one-half mile shoreline of 145 acre Lake Murphysboro offers a variety of outdoor recreation facilities and activities. The nearly three mile ridge and ravine loop of the Walk-Away Trail does just that from the developed shoreline into the northwest portion of the park.

*T*he trailhead begins and ends at the visitor parking area of Big Oak campground. From the campground the trail leads into a maturing mixed deciduous forest and crosses several small draws or tributaries of Lake Murphysboro. The forest path heads uphill to cross the main park road. The Walk-Away Trail may also be accessed here along the pullouts where signs are posted just before the Oak Point picnic area access road. Across the road the trail follows the hillside next to a small meandering stream then uphill to Razor Back Ridge and a trail crossing. Go left and follow the ridge to its end where a rest bench has been provided. A flight of stairs leads downhill from this point along a lowland, looping back to the trail crossing and Razor Back Ridge. Go left following the ridge back across the main park road to descend at the lake and a small bridge crossing. This trail is a full loop. Continue back to the campground. The cool and damp wooded areas of the park are home to nine different types of native orchids. Birders will enjoy the possibility of viewing the spotted sandpiper, swamp sparrow, orchard oriole, pine siskin and a variety of seasonal warblers.

*M*uch of the lake's shoreline is walkable, especially in the picnic areas near the lake such as Oak Point, Lakeshore Drive, Pine Circle, Hickory Grove, Shady Cove, Bald Knob and Clear View. The shoreline of 15 acre Little Lake, north of Lake Murphysboro along the main park road, is hikeable along the fishermen path.

Pine Tree bark

To reach Lake Murphysboro State Park from I-57, take exit #54A-B west onto S.R. 13 at Marion. Go west on S.R. 13 through Carbondale to Murphysboro. The state park entrance is located one mile west of Murphysboro and one mile east of Kinkaid Lake marina and boat launch ramp which is just north of S.R. 149.

32

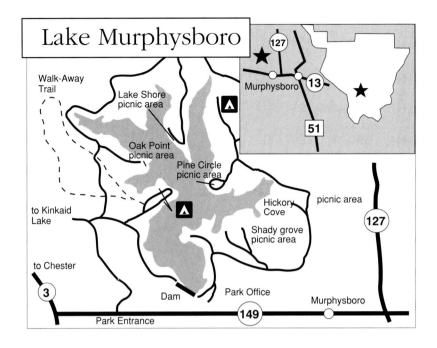

Lake Murphysboro

Walk-Away Trail

Lake Shore picnic area

Oak Point picnic area

Pine Circle picnic area

to Kinkaid Lake

Hickory Cove

picnic area

Shady grove picnic area

to Chester

Dam

Park Office

Murphysboro

Park Entrance

Murphysboro

Lake Murphysboro State Park

• • •

Location:
Murphysboro, IL/Jackson County

U.S.G.S. Map(s):
1:24,000 Oraville

Trail(s) Distance:
three mile loop trail

Activities:
hiking, nature study, backcountry
camping, picnicking, shelters,
playground, lake fishing, canoeing,
10 mph boating, boat launch ramp,
docks, pier, archery range, B–C &
youth camping, concessions,
handicapped facilities

Fee(s):
camping and boat rental

• • •

32

Kinkaid Lake Trail

Great Blue Heron

*T*he Kinkaid Lake Trail is the longest hiking path in the Murphysboro District. The trail follows the southwest shore and ridge along Kinkaid Lake. The lake is located five miles west of Murphysboro, Illinois. Boulders and heavy timber cover the steep 82 mile shoreline. The northwest terminus is located at Johnson Creek Recreation Area east of S.R. 151 and the southeast terminus or State Trailhead is at Crisenberry Dam. The primitive 15 mile forest and lakeside trail are undeveloped except at the main trailheads so bring all necessary supplies including water.

*B*eginning north at Johnson Creek Recreation Area, trailside parking is located alongside S.R. 151 at the entrance to the recreation area. The forest trail follows a small ridge near the main park road downhill from the campground area. Johnson Creek has three miles of loop trail developed within the recreation area. After one mile the trail crosses the footbridge over Johnson Creek through the hike-in-camp and continues south on the ridges 3.25 miles to Hidden Cove Trailhead. This second parking trailhead area south of Johnson Creek Recreation Area tends to be overgrown and the farthest from the lakeshore. Hidden Cove Trailhead is accessible from S.R. 151.

*F*rom Hidden Cove Trailhead, the path continues south 5.9 miles to Buttermilk Hill Trailhead following closer to the lakeshore finger coves. This section is very scenic as the trail skirts between the lake and the exposed sandstone outcrops. The final three-fourths of a mile is a spur ravine-ridge trail heading south to Buttermilk Hill Trailhead from a finger lake cove.

*F*rom Buttermilk Hill Trailhead the shoreline trail goes north and east four miles to Buttermilk Hill Beach and Picnic Area, accessible only by hiking and boat. At one point the trail encircles a projecting peninsula that juts out into the lake. From Buttermilk Hill Beach and Picnic Area it is three final miles to State Trailhead, the southwest trail terminus at Crisenberry Dam. Day trips may be arranged by car shuttle.

J ohnson Creek Recreation Area is the location of the northwest end of the 15 mile Kinkaid Lake Trail alongside S.R. 151 just before the Kinkaid Lake bridge crossing midway between S.R. 3 and S.R. 4. The recreation area offers hiking, picnicking, fishing, swimming beach, boat launch ramp, single-, multi- and hike-in camping.

T o reach Hidden Cove Trailhead three and one-quarter miles south of Johnson Creek S.R. 151 trailhead, go north one and one-quarter miles from S.R. junction 3 and 151 on S.R. 151 to Gum Ridge Road/F.R. 768. Go east on Gum Ridge Road about two miles to where the road curves north and an old service road crossing F.R. 768C. Follow the old service road downhill to the parking area staying to the right of the fork. This access point is not recommended because of road conditions and unsupervised parking.

T o reach Buttermilk Hill Trailhead from S.R. 3 turn north onto gravel road F.R. 718 at the gas station about three miles east of the junction of S.R. 3 and S.R. 156. Follow the curving road northeast turning right at the "T" junction with F.R. 716/718. Go right at the junction about a mile to the marked trailhead on the west side of the road.

T o reach State Trailhead from S.R. 149, located one-half mile north of Grimsby, Illinois, west of Murphysboro, Illinois and east of the S.R. 3 junction about a mile, go north on the paved road along Kinkaid Creek just west of the Kinkaid Creek bridge over S.R. 149, one and one-half miles to the Crisenberry Dam and trailhead parking. The gate may be closed during the winter months but parking for trail hiking is available next to the gate. Be advised this access point is seldom supervised.

33

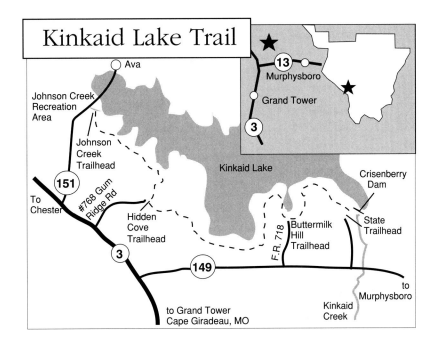

Kinkaid Lake Trail

• • •

Location:
Shawnee National Forest, Johnson Creek
Recreation Area South to Crisenberry Dam

U.S.G.S. Map(s):
1:24,000 Raddle, Oraville

Trail(s) Distance:
15 linear miles one-way, three mile loop
Johnson Creek Recreation Area

Activities:
hiking, nature study, backpacking,
picnicking, shelters, beach swimming,
fishing, pier, boating, boat launch, boat
ramp, marinas, docks, water skiing, seasonal
hunting, camping, concessions

Fee(s):
camping, boat rentals

• • •

33

Cedar Lake Trail & Little Cedar Lake Trail

Little Cedar Lake, west shore

Day hikers and overnight backpackers will enjoy this natural hiking stretch, especially Cove Hollow, Wolf Den Hollow and the west shoreline of Little Cedar Lake. Five and one-half miles of the Cedar Lake Trail from Cove Hollow to Newbolt Site is linear one-way where you must either car shuttle or retrace your steps. The loop around Little Cedar Lake is 4.25 miles. The nearly ten miles of trail follows the west border of the west finger of Cedar Lake, located four miles southwest of Carbondale, Illinois and one mile east of Pomona, Illinois.

Three trailheads are signed and easily accessed from S.R. 127: north, south, and east of Pomona within three miles of each other. The north trail terminus turnoff from S.R. 127 is one half mile north of the Pomona turnoff and one mile east and north of Pomona. Go east 1.2 miles on paved C.R. 17/Dutch Ridge Road, curving east before the Dutch Ridge Baptist Church and Cemetery to the marked right/east turn, and continue one mile more on the gravel road to the dead end at Cove Hollow Trailhead, a total of 2.2 miles from S.R. 127. Parking is available for about five vehicles or so.

The trail heads east towards Cedar Lake and the sign reads one and one-half miles to Wolf Den Hollow. A side spur south at the trailhead goes to Cove Hollow and reconnects with the main trail. The rocky and well-worn main trail follows Cove Hollow and the lakeshore fingers south along the base of a cliff to Wolf Den Hollow. The trail encircles or loops the nearly circular horseshoe-shaped limestone bluff and heads west to Pomona Road and trailhead. The total distance from Cove Hollow Trail head to Pomona Road trailhead is 3.75 miles.

Pomona Road and trailhead are accessed east of the junction of S.R. 127 and C.R. 28, one-half mile south of the Dutch Ridge

Road/C.R. 28 and two miles north of the Newbolt Road turnoff. Directly east of the village of Pomona one-half mil is S.R. 127 and the Pomona Trailhead is about one mile due east from the village. Go east about one-half mile on C.R. 28 to the Pomona Road trailhead, about a half-mile before the boat ramp and road's end at Cedar Lake. Parking is available at the marked pullout for two cars. This central trail access point provides good day hikes either direction north or south. From this central trailhead it is a 1.75 mile hike along lake coves, across creeks, along ravines, hillsides and ridge to the Newbolt access site, the third trailhead and Little Cedar Lake. The Pomona-Newbolt segment provides ideal forest hiking along a narrow earth path through maturing hardwoods.

The access road to the Newbolt Site, the most southern of the three trailheads, is located at the junction of S.R. 127 and the Jackson and Union County Line Road. Go east and northeast just over a mile to the Newbolt Site Trailhead. This access road can be very rough and potholed where it narrows down south of a farmhouse about a mile from S.R. 127.

Little Cedar Lake Loop Trail begins and ends at the Newbolt Site by going east along a service road to the causeway. Cross over the causeway and follow the trail along the lake a short distance. The trail leads uphill through pine plantations out of sight of the lake. ORV use is obvious on this side of the lake. The white diamond blazes are rare in this section and the trail may not be so obvious but it continues to encircle the lake. Cedar Creek is crossed twice. The west shore is well marked and follows the lake shore alongside rock outcrops. Ospreys or fish hawks may be seen flying over the lake in search of prey. Fishermen occasionally ply their boats on the small lake. Arriving at the causeway go left/west back uphill to the Newbolt access site to complete a 4.25 mile hike.

*T*o reach the three Cedar Lake trailheads from I-57, take exit #30 west onto S.R. 146 and proceed to Jonesboro, Illinois. Continue on S.R. 146 to the S.R. 127 junctions just west of Jonesboro and go north. Continue on S.R. 127 beyond Alto Pass, Illinois and at the Jackson and Union County Line turn east on the Newbolt Site Road and Trailhead.

*A*bout two miles north on S.R. 127 at Pomona, Illinois the second trailhead access is found east on Pomona Road/C.R. 28. The third access is about one-half mile north of Pomona Road on Cove Road/C.R. 17 immediately north of Dutch Ridge Church. Consider car shuttles or shorter hikes in selected trail segments.

*Y*ou may also exit from I-57 at exit #54A-B west on S.R. 13 at Marion, Illinois. Proceed west on S.R. 13 through Carbondale to Murphysboro, Illinois and the junction of S.R. 127. Go south on S.R. 127 to Pomona. The three trailhead roads east, north and south of Pomona and S.R. 127.

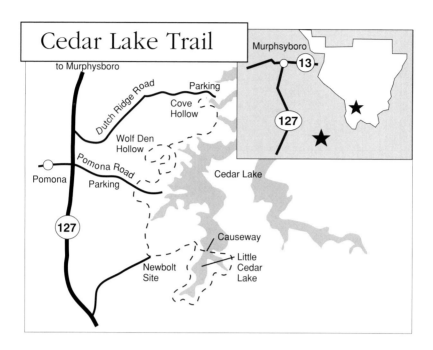

Cedar Lake Trail

to Murphysboro

Dutch Ridge Road

Parking

Cove Hollow

Wolf Den Hollow

Pomona Road

Pomona

Parking

127

Cedar Lake

Causeway

Newbolt Site

Little Cedar Lake

Murphsyboro

13

127

Cedar Lake Trail & Little Cedar Lake Trail

• • •

Location:
Shawnee National Forest, Pomona,
IL/ Jackson County

U.S.G.S. Map(s):
1:24,000 Pomona, Cobden

Trail(s) Distance:
ten miles one-way

Acreage:
1,750 acre Cedar Lake

Activities:
hiking, nature study, fishing,
boating (10 mph max.), boat
launch ramp, backpacking

Fee(s):
none

• • •

Pomona Natural Bridge Recreation Area

Pomona Natural Bridge

*P*omona Natural Bridge is a pleasant woodland ravine setting of picnic areas and trails that lead to a stream crossing through a rock arch "bridge" or joint sandstone block spanning 90 feet across. The natural bridge, one of the few east of the Mississippi River, is formed of resistant sandstone strata. As the water erosion lowered the original stream bed, a remnant of the eroded tunnel became a natural bridge or arch 25 feet above the sculpturing stream. The north side of the bridge was at one time a cliff face. There are overlooks and benches provided to stop, rest and view the rock formation and beautiful ravine surroundings. User-made trails lead under the bridge and along the stream and adjacent bluffs but it is advised to stay on the trail to prevent unwanted erosion.

*T*o reach Pomona Natural Bridge from I-57, take exit #30 west onto S.R. 146 and proceed to the junction with S.R. 127 just west of Jonesboro, Illinois. Go right/north on S.R. 127 about 12 miles to Pomona's village center just one mile west of S.R. 127. Go north on F.R. 750 gravel road about two miles to the Pomona Natural Bridge Recreation Site at the road's dead end.

*T*he recreation site may also be reached from I-57 at Marion, Illinois by exiting 54 A-B west on S.R. 13. Proceed west on S.R. 13 to Murphysboro, Illinois and the junction with S.R. 127. Go south on S.R 127 about ten miles and turn west one mile to the Pomona village center. Go north on F.R. 750 to the Pomona Natural Bridge Recreation Site parking area. The site is approximately two miles north and west of Pomona, Illinois.

*A*pproximately one mile from Pomona at the Cave Creek bridge crossing, locally known as the Cave Creek Valley or Canebrake. This is one of the best areas in the Midwest to see migrating warblers and other migratory birds in late April, early May,

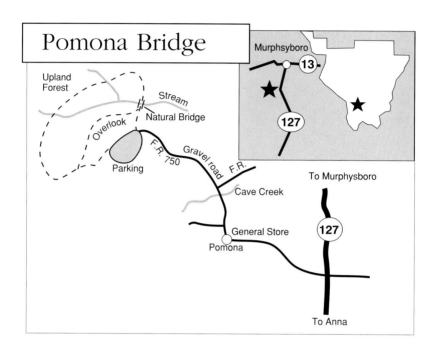

Pomona Bridge

Murphsyboro

13

Upland Forest

Stream

Natural Bridge

Overlook

F.R. 750

Gravel road

F.R.

Parking

127

Cave Creek

To Murphysboro

General Store

127

Pomona

To Anna

August, September and fall. Park on the north side of Cave Creek bridge and walk east along an old forest road.

35

Pomona Natural Bridge Recreation Area

• • •

Location:
Pomona, IL/Jackson County

U.S.G.S. Map(s):
1:24,000 Pomona

Trail(s) Distance:
0.3 mile loop

Activities:
hiking, nature study, fishing,
boating (10 mph max), boat launch
ramp, backpacking

Fee(s):
none

• • •

Little Grand Canyon Recreation Site

Chalk Bluff overlook

*T*he Little Grand Canyon was carved over the centuries by a stream that is a mile-long tributary of the Big Muddy River. At the canyon's head waters, waterfalls flow gracefully over steep sheer walls. Near the streams confluence with the river, vista-rich Chalk Bluff and Swallow Rock rise from the floodplain as much as 230 feet. Plant and animal life are as diverse as the habitats. The plant life accounts for 650 flowering and 27 fern-like species. Many mammal species live in the canyon. Be advised that the sandstone overhangs provide snake dens for copperhead, timber rattlesnake and cottonmouth as well as several non-poisonous species.

*T*he Little Grand Canyon National Recreation Trail is a 3.6 mile hiking loop that ranges in elevation from 350 to 700 feet and is marked both ways by white blazes. The trailhead begins to the right/north of the parking lot and heads west along Viney Ridge on a graveled all weather path. The ridgetop trail turns right/north at Chalk Bluff and continues along the blufftop with vistas of the Big Muddy River valley. At the bluff's end you can see Swallow Rock to the immediate north, the Big Muddy River, Turkey Bayou campground, Oakwood Bottoms, Greentree Reservoir below and Fountain Bluff and Missouri far to the West. The trail turns right/east and follows the hillside to the Little Grand Canyon, descending a water-carved scenic tributary side canyon to the floodplain below. The trail turns right once again and follows the floodplain forest path across small streams to another tributary side canyon. From here the trail heads up through the side canyon. Carved steps cut into the sandstone ledges during the Civilian Conservation Corps' work crew days of the 1930s provide a staircase up from the Little Grand Canyon floor. The final segment heads uphill to the parking area.

*T*o reach Little Grand Canyon from I-57, take exit #54A-B west onto S.R. 13 and drive to Carbondale, Illinois. Continue from Carbondale on S.R. 13 west seven miles to Murphysboro, Illinois and turn south on S.R. 127. Proceed south on S.R. 127 five miles to Etherton junction and turn right/west. Follow Etherton Road southeast about four miles to F.R. 346. From F.R. 346 go two and one-half miles west past Fairview Church to Hickory Ridge Lookout Tower parking area and the adjacent marked trailhead. Follow the directional signs.

*F*rom Murphysboro you may also take 20th Street south approximately one and one-half miles and turn left onto Hickory Ridge Road. Proceed on Hickory Ridge Road about three miles until you reach the first main crossroads. Turn right and continue on the main road about two and one-half miles to the Little Grand Canyon entrance sign. Turn right to the parking area.

*I*n addition you may also take exit #30 from I-57 onto S.R 146 west. Just beyond Jonesboro, Illinois go north at the junction on S.R. 127. Continue north on S.R. 127 to Etherton junction and follow the signs.

*L*ittle Grand Canyon Recreation Site may also be reached from S.R. 3 near Sand Ridge, Illinois by driving 12 miles east and south and from Murphysboro seven and one-half miles south and west. The site lays ten miles north and west of Pomona, Illinois.

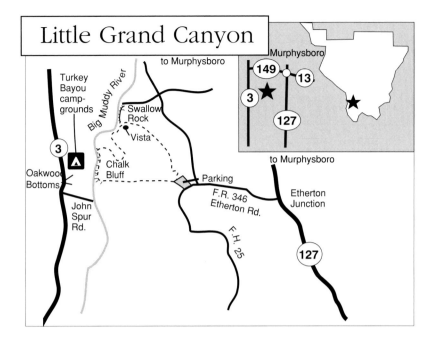

Little Grand Canyon Recreation Site

• • •

Location:
Etherton, IL/Jackson County

U.S.G.S. Map(s):
1:24,000 Gorham

Trail(s) Distance:
3.6 mile loop

Acreage:
1,372 acres

Activities:
hiking, nature study, picnicking

Fee(s):
none

• • •

36

Oakwood Bottoms, Turkey Bayou & Fountain Bluff

Trees overriding Turkey Bayou

*O*akwood Bottoms Interpretive Site is managed by the Shawnee National Forest and lays next to the Greentree Reservoir Waterfowl Management Area established in 1964. The "bottoms" naturally evolved from the frequent flooding of the Mississippi and Big Muddy Rivers that created ponds from the clay sediment. Drainage and levees had reduced these ponds for agriculture and flood control in the early years of settlement however Ducks Unlimited and the Illinois Department of Conservation in cooperation with the national forest service have worked together to redevelop wetlands for waterfowl.

*T*he developed 12 acre site features sheltered picnicking areas, restrooms, small ponds encircled by a paved loop path and a boardwalk loop, both handicapped accessible. Herbaceous wildflower borders and poplar family groves thrive along the edge of the 0.4 mile trail around the small ponds. East of the ponds, path and parking area is the one-eighth mile Walk of Life boardwalk loop that passes through a small portion of the Greentree Reservoir that is partly flooded from October to February to encourage waterfowl, particularly mallards, pintails, American black ducks and wood ducks to seek refuge. Over 80,000 ducks and other migrating birds of the Mississippi flyway pass through Oakwood Bottoms during the winter. The area is also a permanent home for wild turkey, woodpeckers and owls. The wet-mesic floodplain forest includes such oaks of the "bottoms" as cherrybark, burr, willow and especially pin along with other moisture seeking trees: sugar maple, hackberry, sweetgum, American elm, red ash, and kingnut hickory. Oakwood Bottoms is easily accessible from F.R. 786/John's Spur Road and S.R. 3, south of Gorham, Illinois.

*T*hree and one-half miles east of Oakwood Bottoms at the dead end of F.R. 786 is Turkey Bayou campground that is open from

View of the Mississippi River from Fountain Bluff

37

May 1 to December 15. The name "bayou" is derived from the Choctaw Indian word, "bayuk," a body of backwater or tributary to an adjacent stream. The dead end access F.R. 786 allows for a sense of remote wilderness peace in a southern swampland surrounding.

*A*cross the Big Muddy River from Turkey Bayou Campground are the Little Grand Canyon Trail and Recreation Site accessible only by boat from this location. Canoeists may access the scenic Big Muddy River at the carry down canoe or boat access at the campground or the Big Muddy Picnic and Boat Launch Site, uproad about one-half mile from the camp towards Oakwood Bottoms. A popular canoe trip is a 30 mile fluvial journey beginning at Riverside Park in southwest Murphysboro, Illinois floating south past scenic bluffs and winding bends.

*T*o reach Oakwood Bottoms and Turkey Bayou Recreation areas from I-57, take exit #30 and #54A-B west to S.R. 3 and three miles south of Gorham, to F.R. 786/John's Spur Road. Oakwood Bottoms is located one-half mile east of S.R. 3 and Turkey Bayou is four miles east of S.R. 3.

*N*orth of F.R. 786/John's Spur Road about one-half mile on S.R. 3 towards Gorham is F.R. 787 west is easy to miss as it is located between a farmhouse and outbuilding. From S.R. 3, the two to three mile-long rough forest road ascends Fountain Bluff to a prominent Mississippi River bend scenic overlook with room for three vehicles. Vistas of the "Father of American Waters" is worth the drive. You may walk the ridgetop powerline service road in either direction for about a mile for a great river-view hike.

*A*long the Mississippi River side of Fountain Bluff near Gorham, Illinois are prehistoric rock carvings or petroglyphs carved into

Native American petroglyph at Fountain Bluff (at left)

the bluff by early Native Americans. Unfortunately people have carved their own symbols into the sandstone wall, but to view the remaining intact Indian carvings is worth the side trip while in the area.

*T*o reach the rock carving site drive north from Oakwood Bottoms on S.R. 3 and turn left/west onto the Gorham Road just before the bridge crossing. Drive 1.2 miles to Gorham and Second Street and turn left. Continue two blocks to Lake Street, turn left/east and proceed 1.1 miles on the gravel road to the petroglyphs where roadside parking is available. The short trail leading to the rock carving is obvious. If you continue 0.2 miles farther to an old barn there is a waterfall at the base of the bluff.

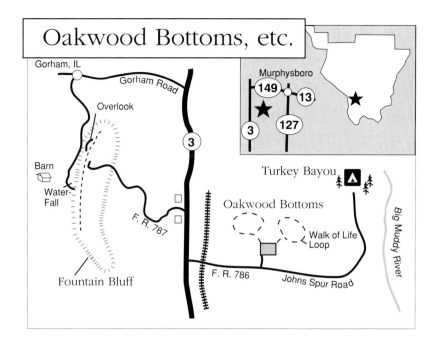

Oakwood Bottoms, Turkey Bayou & Fountain Bluff

• • •

Location:
Gorham, IL/Jackson County

U.S.G.S. Map(s):
1:24,000 Gorham

Trail(s) Distance:
two short trails total one-half mile

Activities:
nature walk, boardwalk, handicapped accessible, nature study, picnicking, shelters, lake fishing, fishing platforms, boating, boat launch, campground (May 1–Dec 15), wildlife refuge

Fee(s):
camping at Turkey Bayou

• • •

Devil's Backbone

Devil's Oven

*L*ocated on the Mississippi River, Devil's Backbone Park was established in 1939 and is administered by the Grand Tower Park District Board. The location of the park is exceptionally scenic due to the sand bar beach strand, the rock formations of the Devil's Backbone, Devil's Bake Oven, Tower Rock near the Missouri shore and the Mississippi River vistas.

A one-half mile graveled hiking trail traverses Devil's Backbone, a high ridge that forms the park's eastern boundary. Access is best alongside the back, east side of the ridge or the north end near the entrance drive. Views are exceptional of the town of Grand Tower, the distant La Rue-Pine Hills, the Mississippi River and Tower Rock, a landmark island of resistant limestone for whom the town was named after and what the French explorers called La Roche de la Croix.

*T*ower Rock is rich in historical lore. Local historian Charles F. Burdick writes that Tower Rock was once called the "smallest national park in the United States." Former General and United States President Ulysses S. Grant saved the landmark from being quarried by setting it aside for public use. It was also the scene of tragedy when an entire wedding party lost their lives in a whirlpool after the engaged couple exchanged vows on the Rock Island. River pirates also stalked the area in the early years of settlement and the ghost of a young forlorned maiden supposedly haunts the shore.

*T*he Devil's Backbone has been severed in two places by road cuts into and out of the park. The backbone was the former site of a brick furnace operated by Grand Tower Mining in 1869. The Devil's Bake Oven lies north of the backbone next to the Mississippi River and just south of the Texas-Illinois natural gas pipeline. The bake oven was so named for the many caves that are

Tower Rock

found around the formation. The stone foundation of an old house is still visible on the east side.

Devil's Backbone Park is located on the river-front in Grand Tower, Illinois approximately one mile west from S.R. 3. Unless you are camping, the park is open from 8:00 a.m. to 10:00 p.m.

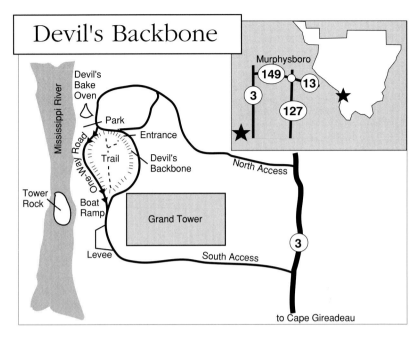

Devil's Backbone Park

• • •

Location:
Grand Tower, IL/ Union County

U.S.G.S. Map(s):
1:24,000 Allenburg, Neely's Landing

Trail(s) Distance:
one-half mile one-way

Acreage:
54 acres

Activities:
nature walk, nature study, historic site,
picnicking, shelters, playgrounds,
volleyball, basketball, river fishing,
boating, boat launch, class A & D
campground

Fee(s):
camping

• • •

"Rest time"

Jonesboro District

Observation Overlook Trails

Inspiration Point area

*T*his unique natural area features a scenic combination of hills with 350 foot high sandstone blufftops overlooking the lowlands of LaRue Swamp and the Big Muddy River and its abandoned old river channels. Within a short distance nature walkers will discover a rich variety of habitats and native flora and fauna. The area contains 1,040 Illinois plant species including 40 species designated as rare by the State of Illinois. Forty mammal species, 24 amphibians, 35 reptiles and 173 bird species also inhabit the area. Several of the plant and animal species are at the edge of their natural range.

*T*he best hike along the base of the Pine Hills bluffs is F.R. 345, especially when the metal gates are closed during the reptilian migration that occurs twice annually. This three-mile section of graveled forest road is closed during the last three weeks in April for the spring migration and again during the last three weeks in October for the fall migration. Motivated by the warm sun of spring, turtles and snakes move from their winter shelters of the talus slopes of the Pine Hills across the road to the LaRue Swamp to live and reproduce for the season. During the waning days of autumn they retreat once more to their winter shelters back across the road. The alarming numbers of road kills induced the forest service to close the road for this annual migration. Hikers are free to explore this section from Winter's Pond picnic area south to the hairpin bend that turns back west. At this point there is a hikeable old road that leads south about half a mile one-way to Otter Pond. Wildflowers are prolific along the talus slopes and adjacent woodlands at the edge of the swamp in springtime.

*A*long the blufftops of Pine Hills there are several short Observation Overlook Trails and vistas of the LaRue Swamp at

Vistas from Observation Overlook Trail

the south terminus. Pine Hills campground is situated in a small, flat floodplain with mature shade trees next to F.R. 236, 0.7 miles north of the Trail of Tears State Forest blacktop, one mile east of Wolf Lake and S.R. 3. The White Pine Trail originates at the Pine Hills campground along with the Hutchins Creek spur trail (see White Pine Trail #41). Pine Hills campground provides water, pit toilets, pond fishing and camping.

*G*oing north on F.R. 236 the next access is Allens Flat, located 2.6 miles north of the Pine Hills campground. Three picnic sites are available as well as pit toilets. Just downhill, north, 0.4 miles, is McGee Hill which provides one of the finest vistas in southern Illinois of the Mississippi River Valley, LaRue Swamp and Big Muddy Bottoms. It is also a fine place to picnic.

39

*C*rooked Tree Trail is 1.3 mile north of McGee Hill on F.R. 236. From the signed pullout, the short 0.2 mile, one-way graveled curving path leads to a bench overlook of the valley. Saddle Hill vista is the next stop north one-half miles from Crooked Tree Trail on F.R. 236.

*P*ine Grove is 0.7 miles north of Saddle Hill. There is a short one-eighth mile gravel path and valley overlook leading from the signed pullout. A fine stand of native shortleaf pine thrives here. The next crest-top overlook is 0.2 miles north of Pine Ridge on F.R. 236 or Government Rock, where an easy one-tenth mile hiking trail leads to an old fireplace and an excellent lowland vista.

*O*ld Trail Point lays 0.2 miles north of Government Rock. There are fine vistas of Bald Knob to the East in addition to the western Mississippi River valley. Between Old Trail Point and Inspiration Point is the west trailhead of the Godwin Trail. It leads into Clear Springs/Bald Knob Wilderness which contains numerous miles of hiking opportunities (see Godwin Trail, hike #40).

*I*nspiration Point is situated 0.7 mile north of Old Trail Point. From the small parking area a three-fourths mile gravel path leads uphill to the exposed bluffs of Bailey limestone to some of the most breathtaking vistas of the LaRue Swamp, Missouri Ozarks and Mississippi Valley. Inspiration Point Trail then leads downhill along dry and narrow ridges to a deep cool ravine. The National Recreation Trail ends at McCann Springs Picnic Area next to F.R. 236, one-eighth of a mile north of Inspiration Point pullout parking. Retrace your steps or follow the Pine Hills Scenic Drive back south to Inspiration Point.

*C*ontinue on F.R. 236 north downhill to the junction with F.R. 345 and turn left/south. Go past the F.R. 345 junction on F.R. 345 to the 0.3 acre Winter's Pond picnic and boat launch area. This spot is a fine place to leave your car and walk the forest road south to Otter Pond and get a closeup look at the LaRue Swamp.

*T*he northern entrance road to Winter's Pond, LaRue Swamp and Pine Hills Scenic Road is reached from S.R. 3 by turning east about four miles north of Wolf Lake, Illinois on the south side of the Big Muddy River bridge crossing and continuing approximately three miles to F.R. 345. After three miles, Levee Road intersects at a "T" with F.R. 345 at the base of the scenic Pine Hills bluffs. F.R. 345 accesses Winters Pond to the immediate south and Pine Hills Scenic Drive/F.R. 236 to the immediate north.

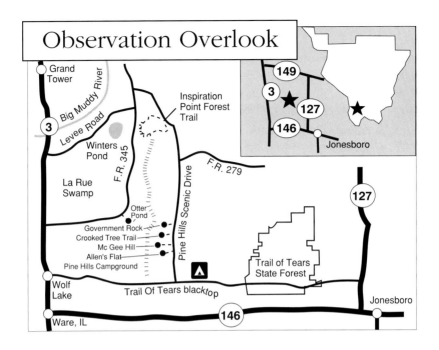

Observation Overlook Trails

• • •

Location:
LaRue-Pine Hills, Wolf Lake,
IL/Union County

U.S.G.S. Map(s):
1:24,000 Wolf Lake

Trail(s) Distance:
1.25 miles

Acreage:
1,372 acres

Activities:
nature walks, nature study, picnicking,
vistas, camping

Fee(s):
camping

• • •

Godwin Trail

Poison Ivy

*T*he Godwin Trail extends six linear miles from F.R. 236 along the Pine Hills bluffs, about one-half miles north of Government Rock and 0.4 mile south of Inspiration Point parking area to Bald Knob blacktop road southwest of Alto Pass about three miles. This is the same road that ends at Bald Knob Cross. Horse riders and an occasional ATV also use this wilderness trail.

*T*he west trailhead begins at the small parking area for four vehicles on Pine Hills Scenic Drive just 0.4 mile, south of Inspiration Point parking area. The trailhead is signed as an access point to the Bald Knob/Clear Springs Wilderness Area. The forest service trail follows the ridge east and south and turns south and west at the second trail heading. This turn is crucial. The first turn south is at a heavily eroded uphill slope and the path south is not conspicuous. The second trail turn is obvious and an unmarked forest service sign is present at the turn. You will know it is the right turn south if you continue on east where the trail forks in 200 yards or so.

*F*ollow the well used ridgeline path to eventually descend at Hutchins Creek crossing. If day hiking this is a good location to consider going on east or possibly north or returning the same route since this is not a loop. If continuing east on the Godwin Trail, the old forest road traverses a lowland area for some distance and eventually ascends a valley to ridgetop that leads to Bald Knob blacktop road which leads to Bald Knob Cross or Alto Pass, Illinois. This portion of the trail can be confusing in places since there are several off trail spurs. Be sure to have a topographical map. Bald Knob Cross comes into view a few places along the trail. Either car shuttle or retrace your steps back to Hutchins Creek and F.R. 236/Pine Hills Scenic Drive.

*T*o reach the east and west trailheads of Bald Knob/Clear Springs Wilderness Trails from I-57, take exit #30 west onto S.R. 146 and drive through Anna and Jonesboro, Illinois. To reach the west trailhead, continue on S.R. 146 to Ware, Illinois and S.R. 3. Turn right/north and proceed on S.R. 3 through Wolf Lake, Illinois north to the highway bridge crossing of the Big Muddy River. Turn right/east on F.R. 324 or Levee Road just before the bridge and follow Levee Road about three miles to the base of LaRue Pine Hills and the "T" junction with F.R. 345 Turn left/north and drive half mile and turn right/east onto F.R. 236 or LaRue Pine Hills Scenic Drive. Go uphill about one-eighth mile to the hairpin turn and the trailhead of Bald Knob/Clear Springs Wilderness Areas.

*T*o reach the east terminus on Bald Knob Road access go north on S.R. 127 at the junction with S.R. 146 west of Jonesboro, Illinois to Alto Pass, Illinois. From S.R. 127 turn west onto Bald Knob Road and drive about 2.7 miles to the Godwin trailhead on the right side of the blacktop road just past the orchard at the road curve. It will require a good day's hike along the 12 mile rugged terrain round trip. Topographical maps are recommended since the trails in the wilderness areas are not signed.

*T*he forest service has recently added a two and one-half mile loop trail in the Bald Knob Wilderness Area south of Bald Knob that begins and ends at Beech Grove Road adjacent to Clear Creek southwest of Alto Pass, Illinois.

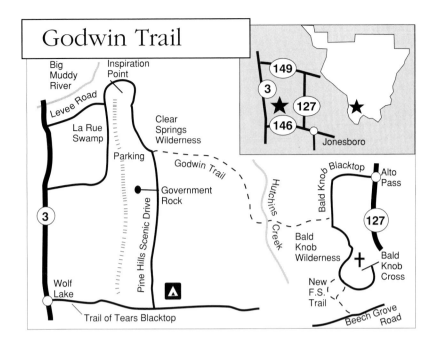

G o d w i n   T r a i l

• • •

Location:
LaRue-Pine Hills Research Natural
Area

U.S.G.S. Map(s):
1:24,000 Wolf Lake, Cobden

Trail(s) Distance:
six miles one-way

Activities:
hiking, nature study, backpacking

Fee(s):
none

• • •

White Pine Trail

Hutchins Creek

*T*hese two long and short linear hiking trails have been laid out in proximity to each other, beginning at or near the Pine Hills campground about two miles northeast of Wolf Lake, Illinois. The trails are used by hikers mainly and are easy to identify and follow however a map is recommended.

*T*he White Pine Trail is a moderate three mile one-way, linear blazed trek that begins at the Pine Hills campground (southwest terminus). The trailhead begins between the two camping sections of Pine Hills campground and is posted. Go east across the small stream uphill to the fishing wildlife pond. Continue the nearly straight uphill trek to the first wildlife meadow opening and cross it staying to the left. In a short time a second wildlife opening will appear containing a large white pine from which the trail's name is derived.

*A*fter the trail enters the forest the White Pine Trail heads left to follow the ridgeline for the remainder of the hike. Finally the trail emerges from the forest at a gate barrier onto F.R. 236 or the Pine Hills Scenic Drive (northwest trail terminus) just south of Allen's Flat. You may either retrace your steps or take the Pine Hills Scenic Drive road to your left and walk over two miles back to the Pine Hills campground to form a complete loop.

*T*o reach the Hutchins Creek Trail spur of the White Pine Trail, continue straight instead of turning into the forest on the White Pine Trail. The trail enters a wildlife meadow then a section of forest and then another wildlife opening and another section of woods. The trail will come to a fork or junction. Go left downhill to Hutchins Creek. You must retrace your steps back to the campground. Both of these trails offer a half-day or more of hiking in the national forest area of the scenic Pine Hills campground area.

*T*o reach Pine Hills campground from I-57, take exit #30 west onto S.R. 146 and drive through Anna and Jonesboro, Illinois to the junction with S.R. 127. Go north/right on S.R. 127 three miles to the Trail of Tears blacktop and turn left/west. Drive through the state forest and about a mile from Wolf Lake, Illinois and S.R. 3 go right/north at the marked forest service sign onto F.R. 236 or the Pine Hills Scenic Drive. Proceed 0.7 miles to the Pine Hills campground on F.R. 236/Pine Hills Scenic Drive at the right/east side of the road.

*F*rom S.R. 3 at Wolf Lake go east about one mile on the Trail of Tears State Forest blacktop to the Pine Hills Scenic Drive on the left/north side of the road. Turn left and cross a small stream dip and drive 0.7 miles to the Pine Hills campground.

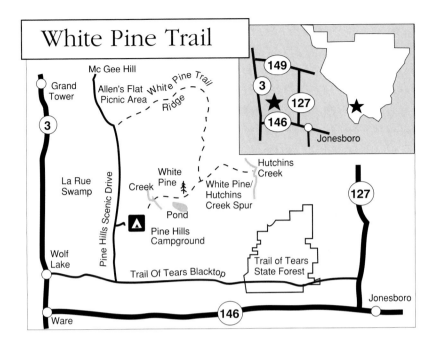

White Pine Trail

· · ·

Location:
Wolf Lake, IL/Union County

U.S.G.S. Map(s):
1:24,000 Wolf Lake

Trail(s) Distance:
two trails total 8 miles round trip

Activities:
hiking, nature study, camping

Fee(s):
camping

· · ·

Iron Mountain Trail

"Sun-forest" in the Morning

*T*his day hike traverses the north-south ridgetop of 700 foot Iron Mountain. The high point provides excellent vistas in all four directions after the autumn leaf fall. During summer the hike is walled in by thick forest vegetation. Old stands of blackjack oak and post oak intermingled with azalea are found along the west facing slope. Iron Mountain was an important site for prehistoric Indians to collect chert rock material for projectiles and other tools. A horseshoe-shaped near loop trail leads down the east slope to encircle a wildlife pond about one quarter mile south of the trailhead. Horses and an occasional ATV use the forest path. The ridgeline trail becomes more overgrown as you hike from north to south along the backbone. Traffic in the valley below can be heard. The trail is not blazed. Retrace your steps back to the trailhead parking.

*T*o reach Iron Mountain trailhead from I-57, take exit #30 west onto S.R. 146 and drive through Anna and Jonesboro, Illinois to the junction with S.R. 127. Go right/north on S.R. 127 about 3.8 miles (about 2.8 miles past the Trail of Tears blacktop) to marked forest road 203 on the right/east side of the highway just before the bridge crossing. Drive one-half mile up the steep hill to the dead-end parking area for six vehicles and the trailhead. The Iron Mountain turnoff is 4.2 miles south of Alto Pass, Illinois.

Iron Mountain Trail

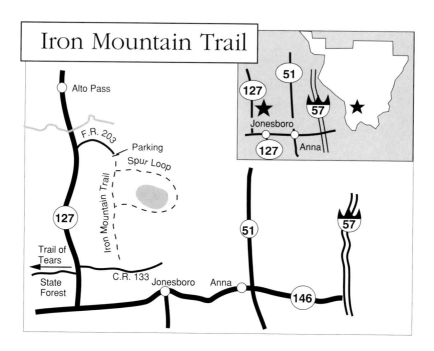

Iron Mountain Trail

• • •

Location:
Kaolin, IL/Union County

U.S.G.S. Map(s):
1:24,000 Cobden, Jonesboro

Trail(s) Distance:
two miles one-way

Acreage:
1,372 acres

Activities:
hiking, nature study, backpacking

Fee(s):
none

• • •

Trail of Tears State Forest

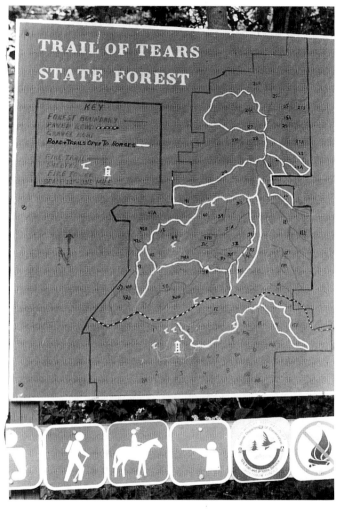

Site map

*T*rail of Tears State Forest was formerly known as Turkey Farm, Kohn-Jackson Forest and Union State Forest over the years. Today's place name is in memory of the 10,000 Cherokee and Choctaw Indians who were ordered to relocate 800 miles from the Appalachian Mountains to a reservation in Oklahoma during the winter of 1838-1839. Movement across the ice-bound Mississippi River was halted and the temporary camps provided little shelter against the harsh winter weather as many died. The Trail of Tears in southern Illinois is identified by historic markers along S.R. 146 from Golconda through Dixon Springs, Wartrace, Vienna, Mt. Pleasant, Jonesboro, Dutch Creek Crossing and Trail of Tears State Forest, ending at Cape Girardeau bridge west of Wolf Lake, Illinois.

*H*ikers may explore the 21 miles of 49 firelane trails that branch off from the blacktop and gravel roads. The north property is the most remote and firelanes #21 to #31 penetrate the long narrow ridges and deep ravines that harbor old growth hardwoods. Hikers may use the designated horse trail in the north property. Divided by the main road blacktop, the fire lanes in the south property are numbered 1 through 15 and north of the road is numbered 16 through 49.

*T*here is also a one and one-half mile hiking trail within the 222 acre Ozark Hills Nature Preserve located in the south property area east of the lookout tower. Fire lane #12 along the South Forest Road is the trailhead for the preserve. A full loop may be hiked by following fire lane #12 uphill from the ball diamond near the picnic area and the State Forest blacktop road to the left/east and then right/west along the South Forest Road to fire lane #5 downhill back to the ball field. A shorter valley spur divides the property.

Lookout Tower

*T*he preserve is characteristic of the Ozarks with its many southern plants, several of which are rare include red buckeye, azalea and cucumber magnolia. The drier upper slopes are covered with oak-hickory forest while the stream bottoms, ravines and north-facing slopes contain beech-maple forest. The preserve provides habitat for scarlet tanager, summer tanager, hooded warbler and Kentucky warbler. Occasionally the Mississippi kite and the bald

43

eagle may be spotted. Geologically, this area is in the Ozark Plateau region characterized by a steep topography and by cherty limestone bedrock that is evident in the stream bed.

Shorter trails may be found in the picnic areas on the south property including one that leads to the fire tower. Although unclimeable, it is the last intact firetower standing in southern Illinois. Visitors will enjoy the unique Adirondack picnic shelters that were built by the Civilian Conservation Corps in the 1930's. Approximately 120 acres of the forest is devoted to the operation of the Union State Tree Nursery which may be toured. The metal gates that access North and South Forest Roads by vehicle are open May 1 to December 24.

Trail of Tears State Forest in Union County is about 40 miles northwest of Cairo, 20 miles south of Carbondale and five miles northwest of Jonesboro, Illinois. From I-57, take exit #30 west onto S.R. 146 and proceed through Jonesboro to the junction with S.R. 127 north. Go north five miles to the junction with Trail of Tears Blacktop connecting Wolf Lake, Illinois and S.R. 3. Trail of Tears Blacktop accesses the forest roads of Trail of Tears.

Approximately 120 acres of the forest are managed as the Union County State Tree Nursery. Ten well-managed acres produce three million nursery stock tree seedlings every year. Tree plantations exist within the nursery and provide high quality seed stock.

Visitors to the area may also want to see the Trail of Tears State Park north of Cape Girardeau, Missouri, the only Missouri state park located directly on the Mississippi River. The 3,306 acre park offers several miles of hiking, picnicking, fishing, swimming, historic sites, a visitors center and camping.

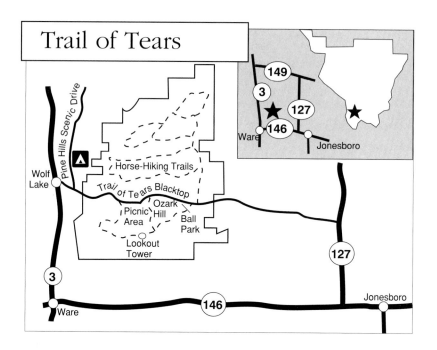

Trail of Tears

Trail of Tears State Forest

• • •

Location:
Jonesboro, IL/Union County

U.S.G.S. Map(s):
1:24,000 Jonesboro, Cobden

Trail(s) Distance:
3.6 mile nature preserve trail also
21 miles of firelanes

Acreage:
5,114 acres

Activities:
hiking, nature study, picnicking,
nature preserve, shelters, ball field,
bridle trails, tree nursery, hunting,
backpacking, tent & group camping

Fee(s):
none

• • •

Lincoln Memorial Site

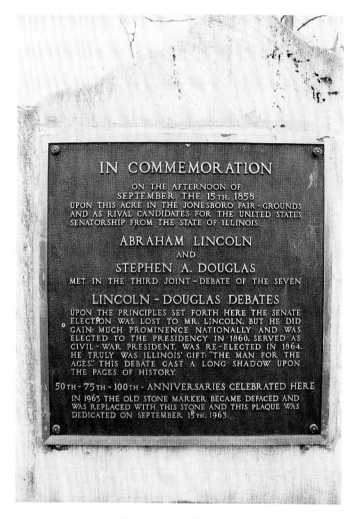

Lincoln Memorial Placque

*A*djacent to the Jonesboro Ranger District Station is the historic site of the third Abraham Lincoln and Stephen A. Douglas debate; the most southern of the Congressional districts where the famous "Sons" of Illinois debated in 1858. Douglas selected Jonesboro, Illinois because it was almost all Democratic and he thought Union County was a position of influence. He was right. A memorial stone honors the September 15, 1858 event, the third of seven debates that covered every section of Illinois through the summer and autumn of 1858. Lincoln and Douglas also debated in the Illinois communities of Ottawa, Freeport, Charleston, Galesburg and Quincy during the late summer and fall of 1858.

*O*ver 1,500 people listened to the political rivals. The people in the audience were not aroused by the slavery question since the issue was not part of their daily lives. Perhaps the highlight of the debate was a display of temper by Senator Douglas, "The Little Giant," who won re-election to the United States Senate that November. The people of Illinois voted to elect members of the State Legislature who in turn elected Douglas for the U.S. Senate. Yet three years later Lincoln was elected President of the United States.

*T*he former forest, farm and fairground tract was purchased by the forest service as an administration site and picnic park in 1936. A short half-mile paved loop encircles the small fishing pond and picnic grounds.

*T*o reach the Lincoln Memorial Site from I-57, take exit #30 west onto S.R. 146 and drive through Anna, Illinois to the Jonesboro town circle or rotary. The site is located one-half mile north of the Jonesboro rotary and S.R. 146, next to the Jonesboro Ranger District Station.

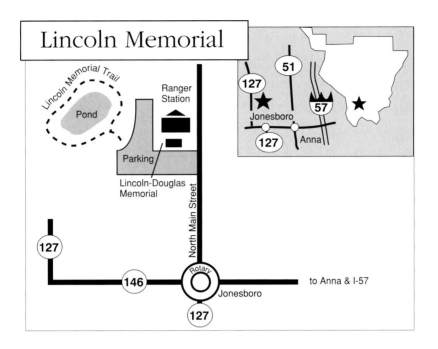

Lincoln Memorial Site

• • •

Location:
Jonesboro Ranger Station,
Jonesboro, IL/Union County

U.S.G.S. Map(s):
1:24,000 Jonesboro

Trail(s) Distance:
one-half mile paved loop

Acreage:
one-half acre

Activities:
Nature walk, historic site,
picnicking, shelter, pond fishing,
playground, restroom, Jonesboro
district ranger station information

Fees:
none

• • •

Hamburg Hill

Heron rookery

*T*he Hamburg Hill Trail is a linear hike that runs along the north side of Hamburg Hill southwest, then south between the level base of Atwood Ridge and the east edge of the Pottsville Bottoms, southwest of Jonesboro, Illinois. The north terminus begins at the junction of F.R. 266 and old county road 649 at a metal barrier gate, northeast of Hamburg Hill and north of the Atwood lookout tower site. Parking is available for four or five cars. The road trail goes west on the old county road 649 descending the hill about three-fourths mile to the Pottsville Bottoms. The trail then follows the base of the ridge south to Upper Bluff Lake's marshy east shore, terminating at Cape Road/Plank Hill Road and the parking area.

*T*he Atwood Ridge area contains the largest stand of rock chestnut oak in Illinois and also has a number of species representative of Appalachia flora including azalea and the magnolia cucumber tree. This is also an area of bird watching for migratory warblers. The lower bluff hike is also very rewarding for bird watchers. Wood ducks are common along the Pottsville Bottoms. Approximately one-half mile north from the south trailhead is a great blue heron rookery. Over 20 nests may be observed during the early spring months. Be advised that the old road trail along the bluff has had heavy ATV usage and the old road trail surface is very rocky in places and has numerous mudholes. The contrast between bluff and wetland makes this a unique and rewarding hike. Retrace your steps or car shuttle for this day-long hike. Be advised that cottonmouth snakes are in the bottoms and mosquitoes and deer fly can be pesky during the warm months.

*T*o reach Hamburg Hill Trail from I-57, take exit #30 west onto S.R. 146 and drive to Jonesboro, Illinois. Continue west on S.R. 146 one mile to the paved Berryville Road just outside

Swimming Cottonmouth

the Jonesboro City limits. Turn south and drive about two and one-half miles to the junction with gravel road F.R. 266. Drive south about one mile to the junction and north trailhead of F.R. 649/Hamburg Hill Trail and park in the available area.

*T*he south trailhead may be reached from Jonesboro by driving south 2.1 miles on S.R. 127 to C.R. 9/Cape Road/Plank Hill Road, north of Dutch Mills, Illinois. Drive 5.3 miles south and west on C.R. 9 along Harrison Creek to F.R. 648 at the road curve between Upper Bluff Lake and Lower Bluff Lake. Turn in and park and hike north across the stream.

*T*he south trailhead may also be reached from S.R. 3 at Reynoldsville, Illinois. Turn east on Plank Hill Road and drive 3.7 miles past Lyerla Lake to the trailhead and parking area.

45

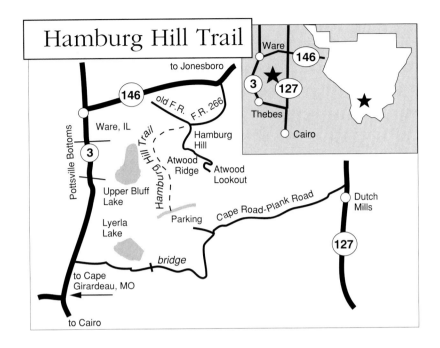

Hamburg Hill Trail

・・・

Location:
Pottsville, IL/Union Station

U.S.G.S. Map(s):
1:24,000 Jonesboro

Trail(s) Distance:
3.6 miles one-way

Activities:
hiking, nature study, backpacking

Fee(s):
none

・・・

Union County Conservation Area

Wetland

*U*nion County Conservation Area is a wildlife refuge for a variety of wildlife, especially 85,000 Canada geese and other waterfowl, wading birds and woodland songbirds which migrate along the Mississippi flyway and winter in the area. Each September Canada geese arrive at the conservation area from their summer breeding grounds in the Hudson and James Bay areas of Canada. These geese are part of the Mississippi Valley population which numbers about 500,000 birds. By mid-March most of them will migrate northward again to complete the annual cycle.

*N*early 1,000 acres are sloughs, marshes, ditches and lakes; 2,500 acres are planted in farm forage wildlife crops and the remaining land is in woodland succession. Three management zones are recognized: refuge area, waterfowl area, and public hunting area. Observation is permitted from the roadway but access to refuge lands are limited. Public use of interior gravel roads is restricted except when permission is granted for special circumstances and events. Check with refuge personnel for current use restriction.

*P*ublic use in the refuge zone is limited to sightseeing and wildlife photography. In order to avoid disturbances of waterfowl in the area, no day use or overnight facilities have been developed. Throughout the fall and winter months, thousands of Canada geese are concentrated along the Refuge Drive, the main road. Few places in Illinois exist where so many wild geese can be closely observed and photographed in their natural habitat. Bald eagles, Mississippi kites, Brant geese and other wildlife are often spotted. For further information about hiking in the sanctuary contact the Site Manager at the Refuge Headquarters on Refuge Road.

*U*nion County Conservation Area north entrance may be reached from I-57 by taking exit #30 west onto S.R. 146 six miles beyond

Lyerla Lake

Jonesboro, Illinois. The north Refuge Road entrance is also about one mile from Ware, Illinois and S.R.3. The south hunting entrance is located just beyond the railroad tracks at Reynoldsville, Illinois about 0.3 miles from S.R. 3. Scenic Lyerla Lake may also be reached from the Reynoldsville access by following Cape Road/Plank Hill blacktop east about two miles from Reynoldsville.

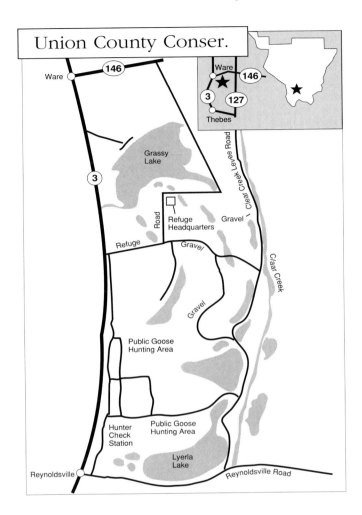

Location:
Ware, IL/Union County

U.S.G.S. Map(s):
1:24,000 Jonesboro

Trail(s) Distance:
road access to sites; no established trails

Acreage:
6,202 acres

Activities:
restricted hiking, nature study, hunting

Fee(s):
none

46

North Ripple Hollow & Pine Knob Trail

Stream at North Ripple Hollow

*N*orth Ripple Hollow and Pine Knob are located in some of the most scenic areas of the Jonesboro District. This moderate to difficult six mile or more hike leads from scenic ridgetops to cool shaded ravines in an area under proposed wilderness inclusion. Trails are poorly signed.

*T*here are two points of access to these areas which also includes South Ripple Hollow and Dogwood Flats. From S.R. 3 at McClure, Illinois, east and north of Cape Girardeau, Missouri, drive east and south 4.6 miles on the Grapevine Trail/McClure-Tamms blacktop to Grapevine Trail campground. Prior to the campground about one-half mile turn left/east on the gravel road that is marked to Mill Creek, Illinois. Drive 2.7 miles to the circular trailhead parking area on the left side of the road that is locally known as the Dago Hill parking area. This road may also be accessed from S.R. 127 just south of Mill Creek at the Union-Pulaski County line by driving west about four and one-half miles.

*T*he second point of entry leads directly to Pine Knob and is located further north and east of the Dago Hill parking area. From the Jonesboro, Illinois town circle, drive 2.1 miles south on S.R. 127 to Cape Road/Plank Hill Road and turn right/west. Continue about one mile and turn left/south on the first gravel road known locally as the Lingle Creek Road. Proceed on Lingle Creek Road about two and one-half miles or more to the F.R. 645 and turn right/west. Follow F.R. 645 about one and one-half miles to the metal gate and park. You are about a mile north on foot from Pine Knob. Please consult the forest service ranger at Jonesboro before hiking this trail. Also, it is wise to carry topographical maps.

*F*rom the Dago Hill parking area the trail curves north along ridgetops that provide scenic vistas of the surrounding hill and dale landscape, especially before the leaves get back on the trees.

The first mile of the trail is a gravel path, the remains of an old county road now known as F.R. 235. The trail "T's" after a mile. Going right the trail turns to dirt and follows F.R. 290 and F.R. 233 to Pine Knob. Going left the trail descends into North Ripple Hollow and leads along the stream that meanders through the hollow to South Ripple Hollow.

*I*nstead of walking a longer loop that leads through South Ripple Hollow and back to the original trailhead, you may shortcut the trail in half by taking the Dogwood Flats Loop. After about one-half mile the trail (which has seen plenty of ATV use) will turn left/south and head upridge about one-fourth mile, and turn east and follow the ridge known as Dogwood Flats to eventually reconnect F.R. 235, the original access trail leading from Dago Hill parking area.

*I*f you continue on North Ripple Hollow, after a mile or so the trail will connect a tributary stream and curve south and east into South Ripple Hollow along old F.R. 230 and F.R. 230A, eventually leading back up the valley to the original access route F.R. 235 and the trailhead.

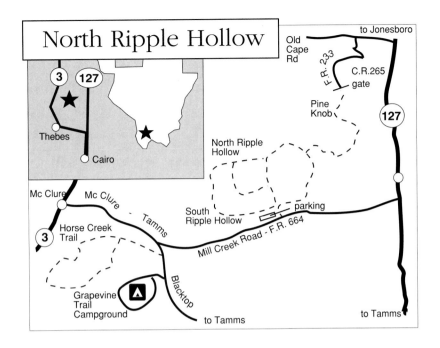

North Ripple Hollow/Pine Knob Trail

• • •

Location:
Mill Creek, IL/Union & Pulaski
Counties

U.S.G.S. Map(s):
1:24,000 Jonesboro, Mill Creek

Trail(s) Distance:
Three miles one-way

Activities:
hiking, nature study, backpacking

Fee(s):
none

• • •

47

Horse Creek Trail

Dogwoods at ridge above Horse Creek Trail

*T*he rugged Horse Creek Loop Trail is conveniently located a short distance north and west of the Grapevine Trail campground. The five mile national forest path follows Horse Creek bottoms south and then west uphill to a high ridge overlooking the bottoms.

*G*rapevine Trail campground is located four and one-half miles southeast of S.R. 3 at McClure, Illinois on the Grapevine Trail blacktop. The site includes six camping spots, picnic sites and pit toilets. No water is available and no camping fee is charged. The trail is marked and obvious.

*T*he Horse Creek Trailhead may be reached from the campground either by walking or driving north on the Grapevine Trail blacktop. Go north from the Grapevine Trail campground 0.2 mile and turn left/west on F.R. 220. Continue west one-half mile on F.R. 220 to the first trailhead that leads to the Horse Creek bottoms on the left/south side of the gravel road. The second trailhead which follows the ridge, is located at the dead-end, another 0.3 mile west on the forest road.

*F*rom the first trailhead the obvious path leads downhill into the valley of Horse Creek. ATV use has kept the trail open where forest service maintenance hasn't. The forest path crosses the stream several times. Spring wildflowers are diverse and abundant in the fertile bottoms. Tulip poplar plantations are reaching a mature size. The trail becomes wider as it enters a clearcut area. Hikers may consider leaving their vehicle at Grapevine Trail campground, since it is a safer site to leave your car for a few hours.

*A*fter a two and one-half mile walk the conspicuous trail heads uphill to the ridge, appear on the right/west side of the path near to a shortleaf pine plantation. The trail goes past a wildlife pond on the left/south. The ridge-top walk is scenic, especially in fall

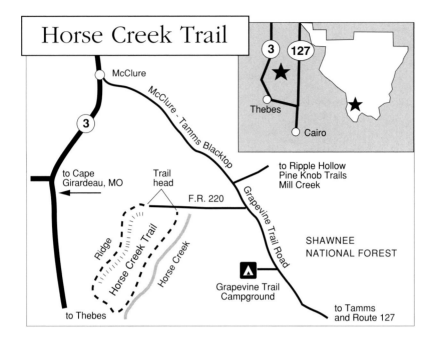

and early spring when vistas are plentiful. Flowering dogwoods are abundant along the east facing slopes in the clearcut area. The trail is actually horseshoe-shaped since it falls about a quarter mile short of forming a complete loop. Go right at the trail's end at F.R. 220 past the first trailhead into Horse Creek bottoms to the Grapevine Trail blacktop and the campground.

48

Horse Creek Trail

• • •

Location:
Grapvine Trail Campground Area

U.S.G.S. Map(s):
1:24,000 McClure, Mill Creek

Trail(s) Distance:
five mile, horseshoe-shaped

Activities:
hiking, nature study, camping

Fee(s):
none

• • •

Sammons Creek Trail

Sammons Creek Trailhead

*L*ocated the farthest trail south of any trail in the Jonesboro District, the Sammons Creek Trail explores a small block of national forest land by following a ridgeline west to east. The second growth mixed deciduous forest is dissected with many deep ravines that provide shelter to wildlife and aesthetic value to the day hiker. The curving clay surface trail is moderately easy except when wet.

*T*he forest trail begins at a roadside pull off at Sammons Creek along Bean Road east of Thebes, Illinois and just east of the residence of a forest service fire warden. The trail immediately crosses the creek and leads to a blue metal gate. Go around the gate and head uphill along the old service roadbed to the ridgetop. The trail follows the ridge and is broken in places by herbaceous wildlife openings. The trail offers fine vistas of the surrounding farmscape during the late fall, winter and early spring months. After two and one-half miles the trail ends at a clearcut and farm field. Retrace your steps west two and one-half miles miles back to your vehicle.

*T*o reach Sammons Creek Trail from Thebes, Illinois and S.R. 3, turn off onto the Gale Road/old S.R. 3 north just south of the Thebes access, and drive 0.2 miles north to Bean Ridge Road. Go right/east on Bean Ridge Road 2.3 miles to the streamside parking pullout and just beyond the fire warden's posted residence where you will see the blue metal gate.

*Y*ou may also access Bean Ridge Road from north of Thebes and S.R. 3 by turning left/east on the posted Gale Road/old S.R. 3 and drive south about two miles, turning left/east onto Bean Road and continuing 2.3 miles to the trailhead.

49

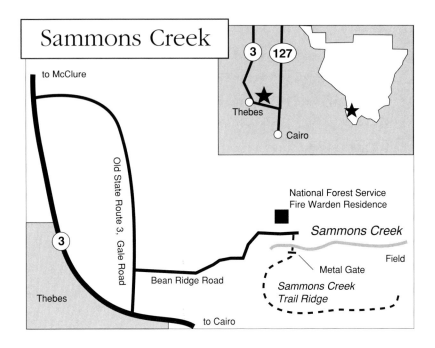

Sammons Creek Trail

. . .

Location:
Thebes, IL/Alexander County

U.S.G.S. Map(s):
1:24,000 Thebes

Trail(s) Distance:
two and one-half miles one-way

Acreage:
1,372 acres

Activities:
hiking, nature study

Fee(s):
none

. . .

Horseshoe Lake Conservation Area

Horseshoe Lake

*H*orseshoe Lake Conservation Area was established in 1927 primarily to serve as a haven for migrating Canada geese. Nationally known as "The Goose Capital of the World," the conservation area serves as a wildlife refuge to 150,000 Canada geese during the cooler fall and winter months. Several bald eagles are also seen at this time. The warm summer months bring many songbirds and waterfowl.

*F*ormed from an ancient ox-bow of the Mississippi River, the man-made lake is so named because of its horseshoe shape viewed from the sky. Horseshoe Lake is unique with its scenic stands of bald cypress, swamp cottonwood and water tupelo dotting the shallow lake along the 20 mile shoreline. "Bucktail fishing" originated at Horseshoe Lake, a name for a cow hair and lead head jig without a bobber that is adapted for the shallow depths of the lake.

*T*here are no established nature trails at Horseshoe Lake; however, the encircling paved park road allows access to the grassy 20 mile shoreline of the large body of water. The best areas to follow the shoreline are along East Side Drive and especially West Side Drive in the picnic and campground areas.

*T*he Horseshoe Lake Nature Preserve has two separate nature tracts that are publicly accessible but do not have established trails. One tract lies south of the Class C camping area bordering the paved road between Miller City, Illinois and West Side Drive along Promised Land Road. Plants that thrive in the wet heavy soils of the west tract include maturing second growth pin oak and sweet gum and the more uncommon cucumber tree, Nuttall oak, willow oak and red buckeye. The second tract is located on the south end of Horseshoe Lake Island beyond the site superintendent's residence at the tip of the island. This hike

Bald Eagle (Forest Service Photo)

50

would require some walking across farm fields. An old growth upland forest of sugar maple, beech, American elm and swamp chestnut oak thrives in this more remote tract which is also populated with Canada geese, green tree frogs, mole salamanders and cottonmouth are some of the amphibians and reptiles found in the preserve.

*T*o reach Horseshoe Lake Conservation Area from I-57, take exit #1 northwest onto S.R. 3 near Future City. Continue on S.R. 3 beyond the junction with S.R. 127 towards Olive Branch, Illinois. Before reaching Olive Branch, three major access roads appear on the south side of S.R. 3: Promised Land Road, East Side Drive and Westside Drive. The main office is headquartered about two miles south of Olive Grove on S.R. 3 along the lakeside of the road. The Miller City blacktop south of Olive Branch accesses the west side of Horseshoe Lake where most of the facilities are located. Horseshoe Lake was designated a National Natural Landmark in 1974.

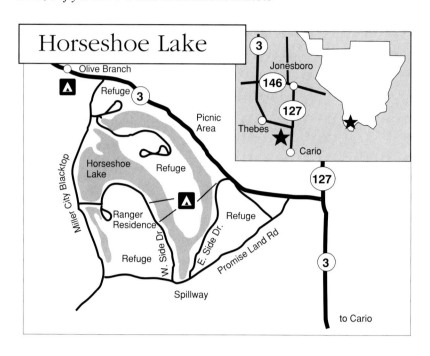

Horseshoe Lake Conservation Area

• • •

Location:
Olive Branch, IL/Alexander
County

U.S.G.S. Map(s):
1:24,000 Cache, Tamms

Trail(s) Distance:
no established distance

Acreage:
10,337acres, 2,400 acre lake

Activities:
walking, nature study, nature
preserve, picnicking, shelters,
playgrounds, ball field, fishing,
restricted boating, boat ramps, boat
docks, seasonal hunting, A-B-C
Campgrounds, concessions

Fee(s):
rentals, camping

• • •

50

Appendix I
Additional Southern Illinois Nature Places

Numbers on the map are keyed to the text that follows.

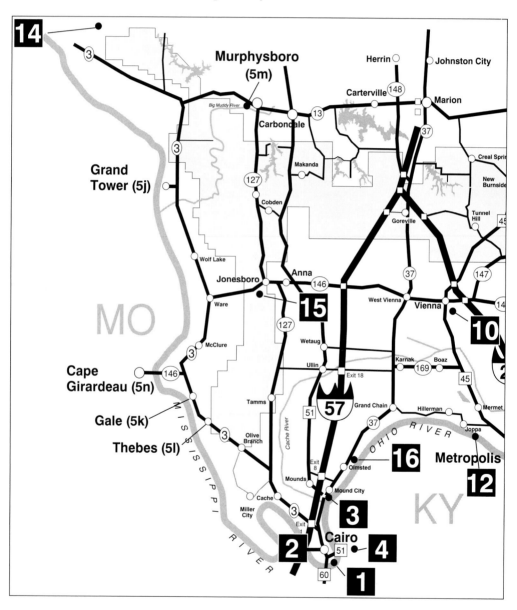

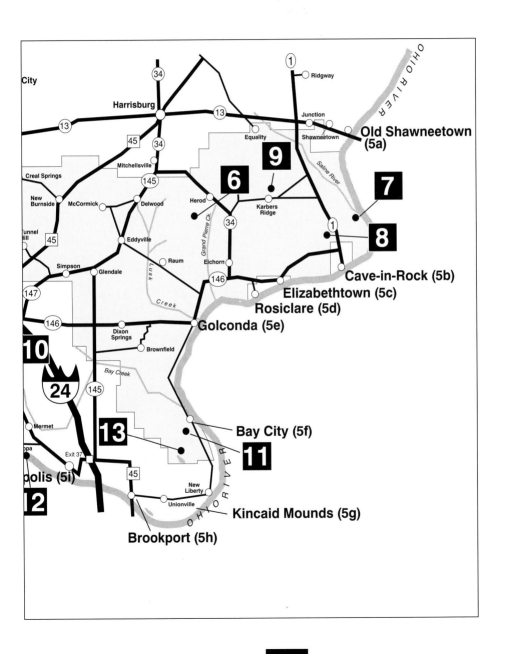

A-I

1 *F*ort **Defiance Historic Site** is situated at Cairo Point, the southernmost location of the state of Illinois where the Ohio and Mississippi Rivers join. The French explorers recognized the importance of the strategic site in the 1670's. The point was particularly important to the Union during the War Between the States or Civil War (1861-1865). Future U.S. President and Union Army General U.S. Grant served here for nearly a year at the outset of the war. Today's visitors may enjoy exploring the vast open spaces of the river's banks and the confluence view from the observation deck of the ship-shaped Riverboat Memorial. The Memorial is dedicated to those who have lost their lives on the river. It also features a concrete-shaded picnic shelter on the ground level deck. It is a great place to gather driftwood. Currently the historic site is leased and maintained by the city of Cairo, Illinois.

*F*ort Defiance Historic Site occupies the land between the bridges of U.S. 60 and 62 that cross over into Kentucky and Missouri. From I-57 at Future City, take exit #1 southeast onto S.R. 3 and proceed about a mile to S.R. 51. Turn south/right and drive about five miles through Cairo to Cairo Point on S.R. 51. The entrance is on the east side of the highway just past the U.S. 60 bridge into Kentucky.

2 *A*nother historic site to visit while in the immediate area is the two acre **Magnolia Manor Historic Home**, Museum and Grounds. The restored 14 room, brick Victorian Home is surrounded by large, white, flowering, gray bark magnolias that lend a festive southern charm. The Italianate-styled mansion was constructed by Charles A. Galigher during the years 1869-1872 after he made his fortune supplying the Union Army with foodstuffs. The site is listed on the National Register of Historic Places.

*T*he home and grounds are open daily 9:00 a.m. to 5:00 p.m. Magnolia Manor is located on Washington Avenue between 27th and 28th Streets in Cairo, Illinois. In addition, Civil War

3

historians may find the **Mound City National Cemetery** of interest. The final resting place of over 2,000 soldiers of both North and South is located four miles north of Fort Defiance near Mound City.

4

*J*ust across the Ohio River at Wickliffe is the **Wickliffe Mounds Archeological Site,** maintained by Murray State University. Wickliffe Mounds is conveniently located across the Ohio River from Ft. Defiance Historic Site near Cario, Illinois and is worthy of visitation for an understanding of how prehistoric Mississippian cultures lived from A.D. 800-1500. Wickliffe Mounds was one of several towns the Indians built along the Mississippi River and its tributary stream, the Ohio River.

*S*ituated at the confluence of two great rivers, the prehistoric Indians established the moderately-sized Mississippian town around A.D. 1100. The community included fields of corn, beans and squash, a plaza where people would gather and socialize, homes of the villagers, a cemetery and mounds for various religious and other purposes. It remains a mystery why the Mississippian culture declined and the town's occupants deserted around A.D. 1500.

A tour of Wickliffe Mounds begins and ends at the visitor's center. The grounds feature a Lifeways Building, Architecture Building, Cemetery Building and a Ceremonial Mound which is the largest mound on the site. Educational displays interpret what is known about the Mississippian culture at Wickliffe Mounds. Recognizing the scientific and educational value of the site, Murray State University continues to study the lifeways and understand the mysteries of the prehistoric culture in western Kentucky.

*T*o reach Wickliffe Mounds from I-57 at Future City, Illinois, exit #1 and drive southeast on S.R. 3 one mile to U.S. 51. Turn south/right, drive about five miles through Cario, Illinois to Cario Point and turn left/east onto the Ohio River bridge. Cross over the Ohio River on U.S. 51/60 and drive about three miles to the outskirts of Wickliffe, Kentucky. The entrance is on the left/north side of U.S. 51/60 just past the Kentucky State Inspection Station at the road curve.

*W*ickliffe Mounds is open daily from March to November, 9 a.m. to 4:30 p.m. Tours and group rates are available by advance arrangement.

5 *S*outhern Illinois River Towns provide a refreshing opportunity to see life along the Mississippi and Ohio Rivers. Nearly all of the towns built along the Ohio and Mississippi River in southern Illinois set aside shoreland for public commerce and enjoyment. Although virtually no maintained nature trails exist, these small acreages of open space parklands provide access to water-related activities and scenic viewing. The gentle terrain of the Ohio River Valley was more conducive for settlement than the larger and rugged Mississippi Valley in southern Illinois. Various levels of government, civic organizations and private individuals have furnished picnic areas, boat ramps, playgrounds, playfields, observation sites, drinking water, restrooms and more along these great American rivers.

*A*long the Ohio River and S.R. 13, **Old Shawneetown (5a)** provides a boat ramp, a large parking area and wooded natural area. Plan on visiting the historic buildings downtown, the site of Illinois's oldest town. Saline Landing, Illinois occupies

Riverboat Ferry

a narrow river terrace at the confluence of the Saline River and Ohio River. Forest Road 1549 penetrates Blind Hollow at the west end of the fishing village. From S.R. 1, two-thirds mile south of Mt. Zion Church north of Cave in Rock, turn east on C.R. 45 and proceed to Saline Landing.

*T*he riverview at **Cave in Rock** (Cave-in-Rock)**, Illinois (5b)** is scenic and the only ferry on the Ohio River has operated for many years, taking passengers and their vehicles to and from Kentucky. The state park provides nearly a mile of shoreline. The town river parks of **Elizabethtown (5c)** and **Rosiclare (5d)** are modern, developed and attractive. Both provide boat ramps, picnicking, shelters, playgrounds and plenty of green lawn.

A-I

Gazebo at Elizabethtown

*D*ownstream at **Golconda (5e)** at the base of Steamboat Hill, the state of Illinois and the U.S. Army Corps of Engineers maintain the full service Lusk Creek Marina. The national forest service provides picnicking and camping at the Ohio River Recreation Area on Steamboat Hill, once the site of the 19th century Rauchfuss Castle. The town of Golconda features a marina and floodwall levee along a lengthy riverside park with boat access and lawn picnicking.

*R*oper's **Landing** and **Bay City (5f)** at the mouth of Bay Creek, ten miles south of Golconda, has a boat ramp and river overlook sites. Hamletsburg is an out-of-the-way rustic river village

18 miles south of Golconda with a boat ramp and camping. Twenty miles south of Golconda is the Smithland Dam and Pool which includes a visitor's center and Ohio River Museum.

*T*he **Kincaid Mounds (5g)** area is located south and east of Unionville, Illinois in south Massac County. The former Mississippian cultural village was once linked to Cahokia Mounds at East St. Louis, Illinois and covered three to five acres. Several mounds are still evident on the Illinois-owned property.

*T*he larger communities of **Brockport (5h)** and **Metropolis (5i)** offer riverside access in their downtowns and at Ft. Massac State Park. Further downstream, both Joppa and Olmstead have boat ramps. Mound City and Cairo have limited access along their river levees but nearby Ft. Defiance State Park provides excellent viewing of the confluence of the two giant streams.

*O*n the Mississippi River, Grand Tower's Devil's Backbone Park is a spacious development in a natural setting north of town. A short trail follows the "backbone" ridge overlooking the river. Downstream from **Grand Tower (5j), Gale (5k)** and **Thebes (5l)** are two historic, closely situated river towns situated on high bluffs. Abe Lincoln practiced law at Thebes and the old historic courthouse provides excellent views of the Mississippi River looking upstream. The river park in Thebes includes a camping area, picnicking with a shelter, boat ramp and playground. Rock Springs is a favorite picnicking spot with natural springs about one-half mile west of the Thebes Spur at S.R. 3.

*M*urphysboro **(5m)**, Illinois is located on the Big Muddy River and the community has established a fine city park along its banks. Recreation facilities include a boat ramp, picnicking shelters, ballfields, a band shell and other resources with plenty of space to walk about.

A-I

*Y*ou may want to consider crossing the Mississippi River at **Cape Girardeau, Missouri (5n)** and explore the community. The Southeast Missouri State University Museum features a permanent collection of Native American Mississippian artifacts and other Missouri-related collections. The University Museum is located in Memorial Hall at the west end of Circle Drive next to Academic Hall on the campus of Southeast Missouri State University. Hours are Sunday 1 to 5 p.m. and Monday through Friday 9 a.m. to 4 p.m. and there is no admission charge. Capaha Park on Perryville Road features a rose garden with over 188 varieties and is a sight to see during the summer months.

*C*ape Rock Park and Twin Trees Park along Cape Rock Drive offers visitor's picnicking along a scenic overlook of the Mississippi River and an opportunity to see southern Illinois from the Missouri side. Hiking trails may be found at Cape County Park at Highway 61 North and I-55.

*I*n addition to the 50 nature walks in southern Illinois there are several places in the region that are available for public visitation however the sites may have little accessibility, require permission to visit and/or have no established trail or other development. The following areas mentioned are by no means a complete listing.

6 *G*yp **Williams Hollow** (U.S.G.S. 1:24,000 Herod) is located just south of Williams Hill Lookout (1,064 feet), the highest point in southern Illinois. The 320 acre crescent-shaped hollow and ridge is a national forest ecological natural area. The hollow is located southwest of Gibbons Creek Barrens Nature Preserve, south of F.R. 404, and south of the Saline and Pope County line west of Herod, Illinois.

A-l

7 *B*lind Hollow (U.S.G.S. 1:24,000 Saline Mines) at Saline Landing is forest service land near the confluence of the Saline and Ohio Rivers. From S.R. 1, go two-thirds miles south of Mt. Zion Church, turn east on CR. 45 and proceed to Saline Landing and Blind Hollow via F.R. 1549.

8 *H*ooven Hollow (U.S.G.S. 1:24,000 Saline Mines) is also Shawnee National Forest land that is not easy to access. One can reach the hollow from the west on F.R. 1749 via C.R. 67 east of Rock Creek Church at the crossroads with C.R. 88. From C.R. 67 Forest Road 1749 is about 1.75 mile to Hooven Hollow with the old road trail following ridgetops and gradually descending northeast to Rock Creek. From the north approach at C.R. 25 about one and one-half miles northeast of Fellows Cemetery on F.R. 1765. The old road descends and loops on the north edge of Hooven Hollow. East along S.R. 1 north of Mt. Zion Church and north of Cave in Rock, Illinois, Hooven Hollow is found a mile upstream from the Rock Creek Bridge. The scenic area was formerly accessible along the now overgrown Anna Bixby Trail from C.R. 67 at the Rock Creek settlement.

9 *P*anther Hollow (U.S.G.S. 1:24,000 Karber's Ridge) is a 180 acre area that includes two hollows in Hardin County. Panther Hollow is narrow and Buckhart Hollow is wider with a seasonal stream. Both have dry upland forest cover and sandstone glade flowering plants. All of the aforementioned nature places are found in the Elizabethtown District.

10 *T*he Vienna District includes some interesting undeveloped natural areas. **Cave Creek Glade Nature Preserve** (U.S.G.S. 1:24,000 Karnak) is owned and maintained by the Illinois Department of Conservation as a dedicated state nature preserve since 1983. The 25 acre limestone glade, upland forest and floodplain preserve is visited by school groups. The limestone glade is one of the best in southern Illinois. A rich variety of prairie grasses and wildflowers flourish at the site. There are no established trails. For further information contact the Natural Heritage Biologist at Ferne Clyffe State Park (618-995-2568). Cave Creek Glade Nature Preserve is located on the east side of Illinois S.R. 45 four miles south of Vienna, Illinois in Johnson County.

11 *C*retaceous Hills State Nature Preserve (U.S.G.S. 1:24,000 Paducah Northeast) needs better access across national forest lands since it is located one mile from the nearest road. The 237 acres preserve unusual acid seep northern plants, especially ferns. The steep wooded hills also support ravine, slope and ridge forest communities. The preserve is also an important historic site. For further information contact the Natural Heritage Biologist at Ferne Clyffe State Park at Goreville, Illinois. The state nature preserve is located near the Pope and Massac County line, one-half miles southwest of Bay City, Illinois.

12 *H*alesia State Nature Preserve (U.S.G.S. 1:24,000 Joppa) was the first nature preserve in Illinois to be dedicated by a private corporation. Access is by permission of the American Electric Power Company. Advise the guard at the Cook Coal Terminal before entering. One-hundred silverbell trees survive within the huge coal transfer facility on the Ohio River, 3 miles northwest of Metropolis, Illinois. The preserve is mostly forested with upland and floodplain trees. For further information contact the American Electric Power Company, Box 428, Metropolis, Illinois, 62960 (618-524-2637).

13 *R*ound Pond (U.S.G.S. 1:24,000 Brownfield, Paducah) is a recent addition of 234 acres purchased by the Illinois Nature Conservancy. This Pope County property is not yet developed for public visitation but future plans include trails and a boardwalk. "Perched" on the ancient terrace of a preglacial lake bed, the unusual bald cypress swamp is believed to be much older than other cypress swamps in southern Illinois.

14 *I*n the Murphysboro District, **Piney Creek Ravine State Nature Preserve** (U.S.G.S. 1:24,000 Welge) is a 111 acre post oak-black oak-shortleaf and pine undisturbed upland forest as well as an 80 foot deep canyon that harbors the northernmost station of beech and tulip poplar. The preserve is located one-half mile northeast of Rockwood, Illinois. No maintained trails exist. For more information about the Randolph and Jackson County Preserve contact the Site Superintendent of the Randolph County Conservation Area. (618-826-2706).

*T*rue explorers will find the national forest lands of Reeds Canyon and Cedar Bluffs difficult to access but worthy of discovery.

*W*ithin the Jonesboro District is the national forest 535 acre Ozark Hill Prairie Natural Area (U.S.G.S. 1:24,000 Olmsted) located not far from the Mississippi River in Alexander County.

15 *B***rown Barrens Nature Preserve** (U.S.G.S. 1:24,000 Jonesboro), **Berryville Shale Glade Nature Preserve** (U.S.G.S. 1:24,000 Jonesboro) and **McClure Shale Glade Nature Preserve** (U.S.G.S. 1:24,000 Jonesboro) are the only three known sites that support shale barrens in Illinois. These rare preserves support stunted trees and herbaceous plants due to a lack of moisture and soil deficiencies. Totaling about 110 acres, these three Union County barrens are located a few miles apart, just west of Jonesboro, Illinois. For further information contact the Natural Heritage Biologist at Ferne Clyffe State Park, Goreville, Illinois (618-995-2568).

16 C**hestnut Hills State Nature Preserve** (U.S.G.S. 1:24,000 Olmsted) is a 212 acre botanical site that lacks public access since it is enclosed by private lands. The preserve's name is derived from the fact that the site supported native American chestnut, however, the chestnut blight has eliminated most of the trees. Significant natural features of the preserve include geological formations and rare and endangered plants and animals such as silverbells, dusky salamander and seasonal bald eagles. The nature preserve is located one-half mile east of Olmsted, Illinois on the Ohio River. For further information contact the Natural Heritage Biologist at Ferne Clyffe State Park, Goreville, Illinois (618-995-2568).

Author standing on 1,000 year-old cypress tree in the Cache River Natural Preserve

Helpful Books

Allen, John W. *It Happened in Southern Illinois.* Carbondale, IL: Southern Illinois University Press, 1968.

Allen, John W. *Legends and Lore of Southern Illinois.* Carbondale, IL: Southern Illinois University Press, 1963.

American Medical Association. *Handbook of First Aid and Emergency Care.* New York, NY: Random House, 1980.

Angel Heather and Wolseley, Pat. *The Water Naturalist.* New York, NY: Facts on File, 1982.

Barton, Cyril. *As the Tree Grows.* Sesser, IL: The Print Shop, 1983.

Black, Harry G. *Trails to Illinois.* Hammond, IN: HMB Publications, 1982.

Bonnell, Clarence. *The Illinois Ozarks.* self-published: 1946.

Borror, Donald J. and White, Richard E. *A Field Guide to the Insects.* Boston, MA; Houghton Mifflin Company, 1970.

Brown, Vinson. *Knowing the Outdoors in the Dark.* New York, NY: Macmillan Publishing, 1972.

Brown, Vinson. *Reading the Woods.* New York, NY: Macmillan Publishing, 1969.

Brown, Vinson. *The Amateur Naturalists's Handbook.* New York, NY: Prentice-Hall, 1980.

Buchholtz, K. P., Grisgby, B. H., Lee, O. C., et al. *Weeds of the North Central States.* Champaign, IL: Agriculture Experiment Station, 1952.

Bull, John, and Farrand, John. *The Audubon Society Field Guide to North American Birds: Eastern Region.* New York, NY: Alfred Knopf, 1977.

Bull, Alvin T., and Runkel, Sylvan T. *Wildflowers of Illinois Woodlands.* Des Moines, IA: Wallace Homestead Books, 1979.

Burt, William H. and Grossenheider, Richard E. *A Field Guide to the Mammals.* Boston, MA: Houghton Mifflin Company, 1969.

Caraway, Charles. *Foothold on a Hillside: Memories of a Southern Illinoisan.* Carbondale, IL: Southern Illinois University Press, 1986.

Center for Archaeology. *The Prehistoric Peoples of Southern Illinois.* Carbondale, IL, 1986.

Conant, Roger. *Peterson Field Guide to Reptiles and Amphibians of the United States and Canada.* Boston, MA: Houghton Mifflin Company. (latest edition)

Culen, Jerry and Hungerford, Harold. *Birder's Guide to Southern Illinois.* Carbondale, IL: Touch of Nature, 1988.

Federal Writers Project. *The WPA Guide to Illinois.* New York: Pantheon Press reprint, 1983.

Fensom, Rod and Foreman, Julie. *Illinois: Off the Beaten Path: A Guide to Unique Places.* Chester, CT: Globe Pequot, 1987.

Fletcher, Colin. *The Complete Walker III.* New York, NY: Alfred Knopf, 1984.

Forbes, Stephen A., and Richardson, Robert Earl. *The Fishes of Illinois.* Springfield, IL: State of Illinois, 1920.

Golden Guide Series. Racine, WI: Golden Press.

Harris, Stanley E., Harrell, William C., and Irwin, Daniel. *Exploring the Land and Rocks of Southern Illinois: A Geological Guide.* Carbondale, IL: Southern Illinois University Press, 1977.

Henbest, Nigel. *A Spotter's Guide to the Night Sky.* Mayflower Books, 1979.

Herkert, James R. *Endangered and Threatened Species of Illinois.* Illinois Dept. Conservation, Springfield, IL, 1991.

Hoffmeister, Donald F., and Mohr, Carl O. *Fieldbook of Illinois Mammals.* New York: Dover Publications, Inc., 1972.

Harrell, C. W., et al. *Land Between the Rivers: The Southern Illinoisian Country.* Carbondale, IL: Southern Illinois University Press, 1977.

Illinois Humanities Council and the National Endowment for the Humanities.Southern Illinois History Inventory. Sponsored bv the Shawnee Library System. Carterville, IL, 1983.

Kals, W. S. *The Stargazer's Bible.* New York, NY: Doubleday, 1980.

King, Frances B. Plants, People and Paleoecology: Biotic Communities and Aboriginal Plant Usage in Illinois. Illinois State Museum, Scientific Papers, Vol. 20, Springfied, IL, 1984.

Kleen, Veron M. and Bush, Lee. *A Field List of the Birds of Southern Illinois.* Carbondale, IL, 1871.

Klots, Alexander B. *A Field Guide to the Butterflies.* Boston, MA: Houghton Mifflin Company, 1951.

Klots, Elsie B. *Freshwater Life.* New York, NY: G. P. Putnam & Sons, 1966.

McFall, D. *A Directory of Illinois Nature Preserves.* Ilinois Dept. of Conservation, Division of Natural Heritage. Springfield, IL, 1991.

MacFarlan, Alan. *Exploring the Outdoors With Indian Secrets.* Harrisburg, PA: Stackpole Books, 1982.

Martin, Laura C. *Wildflower Folklore.* Charlotte, NC: East Woods Press, 1984.

Mohlenbrock, Robert, H. and Voit, J. W. *Flora of Southern Illinois* Carbondale, IL, Southern Illinois Press.

Mohlenbrock, Robert, H. *Spring Woodland Wildflowers of Illinois.* Illinois Dept. Conservation, Division of Forestry, Springfield, IL, 1980.

Mohlenbrock, Robert, H. *Wildflowers of Fields, Roadsides and Open Habitat of Illinois.* Illinois Dept. Conservation, Division of Forest Resources and Natural Heritage, Springfield, IL, 1981.

Neely, Charles *Tales and Songs in Southern Illinois.* Herrin, IL: Crossfire, 1989.

Smith, Phillip Wayne. *The Amphibians and Reptiles of Illinois* Urbana Illinois Department of Registration and Education, Natural Survey Division, 1961.

Thomas, Bill. *Talking With the Animals.* New York, NY: William Morrow & Company, 1985.

Thomas, Lowell J. and Sanderson, Jay L. *First Aid for Backpackers and Campers.* New York, NY: Holt, Rinehart, and Winston, 1978.

University of Illinois Agricultural Circular 718. *Weeds of the North Central States.* Urbana: rev. ed.

Voit, J. W. and Mohlenbrock, Robert, H. *Plant Communities of Southern Illinois.* Carbondale, IL: Southern Illinois University Press, 1964.

Vogel, Virgil J. *Indian Place Names in Illinois.* Springfield, IL: Illinois State Historical Library, 1963.

Watts, May T. *The Winter Tree Finder.* Nature Study Guild, 1963.

Zyznieuski, Walter G. and Zyznieuski, George S. *Illinois Hiking and Backpack Trails.* Carbondale, IL: Southern Illinois University Press, 1985.

Animals of Southern Illinois

*Some common amphibians and reptiles of the
LaRue-Pine Hills Ecological Area compiled from the
Shawnee National Forest listing.*

Turtles

Common Snapping Turtle
Eastern Box Turtle
Eastern Painted Turtle
Red-eared Turtle
Spiny Softshell Turtle

Snakes

Black Racer
Black Rat Snake
Copperhead
Diamond-Backed Water Snake
Eastern Garter Snake
Eastern Hognose Snake
Eastern Rough Green Snake
King Snake
Midland Brown Snake
Midland Water Snake
Midwest Worm Snake
Northern Copperbelly Water Snake
Northern Red-Bellied Snake
Red Milk Snake
Ringneck Snake
Western Ribbon Snake
Western Earth Snake
Western Mud Snake
Western Cottonmouth

Salamaders/Newts/Lizards/Skinks

Broadheaded Skink
Cave Salamander
Central Newt
Ground Skink
Five-Line Skink
Long-Tailed Salamander
Marbled Salamander
Northern Fence Lizard
Ozark Red-Backed Salamander
Slimy Salamander
Small-Mouthed Salamander
Spotted Salamander
Stinkpot
Western Lesser Siren

Frogs/Toads

American Toad
Blanchard's Cricket Frog
Bullfrog
Chorus Frog
Eastern Grey TreeFrog
Fowler's Toad
Green Frog
Northern Spring Peeper
Southern Leopard Frog

Birds of the Shawnee National Forest. Of the more than 650 species of birds found in the United States and Canada, more than 237 are listed here as residents, migrants or frequent visitors to the Forest.

*Threatened, endangered or unique species

*Bald Eagle
*Barn Owl
*Brewer's Blackbird
*Brown Creeper
*Cooper's Hawk
*Forster's Tern
*Great Blue Heron
*Least Tern
*Little Blue Heron
*Long-eared Owl
*Mississippi Kite
*Osprey
*Red-shouldered Hawk
*Sharp-shinned Hawk
*Snowy Egret
*Wilson's Phalarope

Acadian Flycatcher
American Bittern
American Coot
American Golden Plover
American Goldfinch
American Kestrel
American Redstart
American Robin

American Wigeon
American Woodcock

Bachman's Sparrow
Bank Swallow
Barn Swallow
Barred Owl
Bay-breasted Warbler
Bell's Vireo
Belted Kingfisher
Bewick's Wren
Black and White Warbler
Black Duck
Black Tern
Black Vulture
Black-billed Cuckoo
Black-crowned Night Heron
Black-throated Blue Warbler
Black-throated Green Warbler
Blackburnian Warbler
Blackpoll Warbler
Blue Grosbeak
Blue Jay
Blue-gray Gnatcatcher
Blue-winged Teal
Blue-winged Warbler
Bobolink
Bobwhite

A-III

Bonaparte's Gull
Broad-winged Hawk
Brown Thrasher
Brown-headed Cowbird
Bufflehead

Canada Goose
Canada Warbler
Canvasback
Cardinal
Carolina Chickadee
Carolina Wren
Caspian Tern
Cedar Waxwing
Cerulean Warbler
Chestnut-sided Warbler
Chimney Swift
Chipping Sparrow
Chuck-will's Widow
Cliff Swallow
Common Crow
Common Flicker
Common Gallinule
Common Goldeneye
Common Grackle
Common Loon
Common Merganser
Common Nighthawk
Common Snipe
Common Tern
Common Yellowthroat
Connecticut Warbler

Dark-eyed Junco
Dickcissel
Downy Woodpecker

Eastern Bluebird

Eastern Kingbird
Eastern Meadowlark
Eastern Phoebe
Eastern Wood Pewee
Evening Grosbeak

Ferruginous Hawk
Field Sparrow
Fish Crow
Fox Sparrow
Franklin's Gull

Gadwall
Golden-crowned Kinglet
Golden-winged Warbler
Grasshopper Sparrow
Gray Catbird
Gray-cheeked Thrush
Great Crested Flycatcher
Great Egret
Great Horned Owl
Greater Yellowlegs
Green Heron
Green-winged Teal

Hairy Woodpecker
Harris Sparrow
Henslow's Sparrow
Hermit Thrush
Herring Gull
Hooded Merganser
Hooded Warbler
Horned Grebe
Horned Lark
House Sparrow
House Wren

Indigo Bunting

Kentucky Warbler
Killdeer
King Rail

Lapland Longspur
Lark Sparrow
Least Bittern
Least Flycatcher
Least Sandpiper
LeConte's Sparrow
Lesser Scaup
Lesser Yellowlegs
Lincoln's Sparrow
Loggerhead Shrike
Long-billed Marsh Wren
Louisiana Water-thrush

Magnolia Warbler
Mallard
Marsh Hawk
Merlin
Mockingbird
Mourning Dove
Mourning Warbler

Nashville Warbler
Northern Oriole
Northern Parula
Northern Shoveler
Northern Waterthrush

Olive-sided Flycatcher
Orange-crowned Warbler
Orchard Oriole
Ovenbird

Palm Warbler
Pectoral Sandpiper

Philadelphia Vireo
Pied-billed Grebe
Pileated Woodpecker
Pine Siskin
Pine Warbler
Pintail
Prairie Warbler
Prothonotary Warbler
Purple Finch
Purple Martin

Red-bellied Woodpecker
Red-breasted Merganser
Red-breasted Nuthatch
Red-eyed Vireo
Red-headed Woodpecker
Red-tailed Hawk
Red-throated Loon
Red-winged Blackbird
Redhead
Ring-billed Gull
Ring-necked Duck
Rock Dove
Rose-breasted Grosbeak
Rough legged Hawk
Rough-winged Swallow
Ruby-crowned Kinglet
Ruby-throated Hummingbird
Ruddy Duck
Ruffed Grouse
Rufous-sided Towhee
Rusty Blackbird

Savannah Sparrow
Scarlet Tanager
Screech Owl
Semi-palmated Plover
Semi-palmated Sandpiper

Short-billed Dowitcher

Short-billed Marsh Wren

Short-eared Owl

Snow Goose

Solitary Sandpiper

Solitary Vireo

Song Sparrow

Sora Rail

Spotted Sandpiper

Starling

Summer Tanager

Swainson's Thrush

Swainson's Warbler

Swamp Sparrow

Tennessee Warbler

Tree Sparrow

Tree Swallow

Tufted Titmouse

Turkey

Turkey Vulture

Upland Sandpiper

Veery

Vesper Sparrow

Virginia Rail

Warbling Vireo

Water Pipit

Western Meadowlark

Whip-poor-will

White-breasted Nuthatch

White-crowned Sparrow

White-eyed Vireo

White-fronted Goose

Willow Flycatcher

Wilson's Warbler

Winter Wren

Wood Duck

Wood Thrush

Worm-eating Warbler

Yellow Crowned Night Heron

Yellow Warbler

Yellow-bellied Flycatcher

Yellow-bellied Sapsucker

Yellow-billed Cuckoo

Yellow-breasted Chat

Yellow-rumped Warbler

Yellow-throated Vireo

(From *Check List of Birds of Southern Illinois* by Dr. William George, through the U.S. Shawnee National Forest Service.)

A-III

Index

Allen's Flat, 222
Amphibians, 292
Animals, 292
Anvil Rock, 41
Attucks Park in Carbondale, 167

Balanced Rock, **94**
Bald Eagle, 269, 270
Bald Knob Cross, 227
Bay City, 280
Bay Creek, 88
Beaver Trail, 31, **50-54**
Bell Smith Springs, **84-91**
Berryville Shale Glade Nature Preserve, 285
Big Creek Trail, 63
Big Muddy, 211, 219
Big Rocky Hollow Trail at Ferne Clyffe, 150, 151
Birds, 293-296
Books, 288-291
Brown Barrens Nature Preserve, 285-286
Blackjack Oak Trail at Ferne Clyffe, 151
Blind Hollow, 283
Bluff Trail, 107, 109
Boss Island, 110, 113
Brockport , 281
Burden Falls, 89
Buttermilk Hill Trailhead, 191, 192

Cache River, ix, 10, 110, 123, 124
Cache River Natural Area, 111, 115, 117
Camel Rock, 41
Camp Cadiz, 51
Canada Geese, 159, 160, 253, 269
Cape Girardeau, 282
Cape Rock Park, 282
Carbondale, **166-173**
Carbondale Park District, 167
Cave Creek Glade Nature Preserve, 284
Cave Hill Trail, 23, 25
Cave in Rock, **70-75**, 278, 279

Cedar Lake Trail, **194-199**
Chestnut Hills State Nature Preserve, 286
Chimney Rock, 41
Cove Hollow Trailhead, 195
Crab Orchard National Wildlife Refuge, **158-165**
Cretaceous Hills State Nature Preserve, 284
Cuesta, viii-x
cypress trees, 123

Devils Backbone Park, **214-217**
Devils Kitchen Lake, 159, 161
Devil's Smoke Stack, 41
Devil's Standtable Nature Trail, 181
Dixon Springs, **106-109**
Dogwood Flats loop, 258
Douglas, Stephen A. 245
Doug Lee Park in Carbondale, 167
Dutchman Lake, **144-147**

Elizabethtown, 279
Evergreen Park in Carbondale, 168

Ferne Clyffe Lake, 151, 152, 154
Ferne Clyffe Lake Trail, 153
Ferne Clyffe State Park, **147-155**
Fort Defiance Historic Site, 276
Fort Massac Forest Nature Preserve, 137
Fort Massac State Park, **134-139**
Fountain Bluff, 211, 212
French and Indian War, 135

Garden of the Gods, **41-45**
George Rogers Clark, 135, 137
Ghost Dance Canyon Trail, 107, 108
Giant City Nature Trail, 181
Giant City State Park, **180-185**
Gibbons Creek Barrens, **46-49**
Glendale Recreation Area, 102-105
Glen O. Jones Lake, 23
Godwin Trail, **226-229**
Golconda, 280

ID

Grand Tower's Devil's Backbone Park, 281
Grapevine Trail Campground, 261
Green Earth I, II Woodland Preserves, 170, 171
Greenway/Bikeway in Carbondale, 167
Gyp Williams Hollow, 282

Halesia State Nature Preserve, 284
Hamburg Hill Trail, **248-251**
handicapped accessiblility, 5
Happy Hollow Backpack Trail at Ferne Clyffe Trail, 153
Hawk's Cave Trail at Ferne Clyffe, 151
Heron Pond, **116-121**
Heron Pond Nature Preserve, **116-121**
Heron Pond Trail, 117-119
Hickory Nut Trail, 137
Hickory Ridge Loop Trail, 71
Hidden Cove Trailhead, 191, 192
High Knob, **36-39**
hiking Clothing, 4
hiking Gear, 4-5
hiking skills, 3
Hoven Hollow, **283**
Horse Creek Loop Trail, **260-263**
Horseshoe Lake Conservation Area, **268-273**
Hutchins Creek Trail, spur of the Iron Mountain Trail, **234-237**

Illinois State Geological Survey, 6
Indian Creek Shelter and Nature Trail, 181, 182
Indian Kitchen Trail, 79
Indian Wall, 31
insects, 7
Inspiration Point Trail, 223
Interior Highlands, viii
Iron Funace, **62-65**

Jackson Hollow, **92-97**
Johnson Creek Recreation Area, 191, 192
Jonesboro Ranger District Station, 245

Kinkaid Lake Trail, **190-193**
Kincaid Mounds, 281

Lake Glendale, **102-105**

Lake Glendale Trail, 103
Lake of Egypt, **139-143**
Lake of Egypt Recreation Area, **140-143**
Lake Murphysboro, 186
Lake Murphysboro State Park, **186-189**
Lake Trail, 23, 25
LaRue Swamp, 221-222, 224
Lenus Turley Park in Carbondale, 168
LIFE Community Center in Carbondale, 168
Limekiln Springs Trail, **126-129**
Lincoln Memorial Site, **244-247**
Little Bay Creek, 93
Little Black Slough, 111
Little Cedar Lake Loop Trail, 196, 197
Little Grand Canyon, **204-207**
Little Grand Canyon National Recreation Trail, **204-207**
Little Grassy Lake, 159, 161, 175, 176
Little Grassy State Fish Hatchery, 162, 163
Look Out Point Trail, 111
Lusk Creek, 80
Lusk Creek Canyon, **78-83**
Lusk Creek Wilderness Area, **78-83**
Lyme Disease, 7

Magnolia Manor Historic Home, 276
McClure Shale Glade Nature Preserve, 285
Mermet Flatwoods Loop Trail, 131
Mermet Lake, 131-133
Mermet Lake Conservation Area, **130-133**
Metropolis, 281
Millstone Bluff, **98-101**
Mississippian Indians, 19, 99, 277
Mississippi River, 210, 215
morel mushroms, 136
mosquito, 8
Mushroom Rock, 41, 42
Museum State Trailhead, 192

Natural Bridge at Bell Smith Springs, 86, 87
Natural Bridge Trail, 87
Newbolt Site, 196
Noah's Ark, 41, 42
North Ripple Hollow Trail, **256-259**

ID

Oakdale Park in Carbondale, 167
Oak Tree Trail, 107
Oakwood Bottoms, **209-213**
Observation Overlook Trails, **220-225**
Observation Trail, 41
Old Salt Spring, 19
Old Shawneetown, 278
Old Trail Point, 223
One Horse Gap, 58, 59
Ozarks, viii, 2

Paleo Indians, 99
Panther Hollow, 283, 284
Parrish Park, 168
Pine Hills, 219, 220
Pine Hills Scenic Drive, 227, 229, 231
Pine Knob, 257
Pine Tree Trail, 107, 109
Piney Creek Ravine State Nature
    Preserve, 285
Pirate Bluff Trail, 73
poison ivy, 10
Pomona Natural Bridge, **200-203**
Post Oak Trail, 181
Pounds Hollow, **30-34**, 53

Rebman Trail at Ferne Clyffe, 148, 149,
    151
Red Cedar Trail Loop, 183, 184
Refuge, **158-165**
reptile migration, 221
Reptiles, 292
Rim Rock Forest Trail, **31-34**
Rim Rock National Recreation Trail, 54
River-to-River Trail, **56-61**
River Towns, 278
Rocky Bluff Trail, 158, 162
Roper's Landing, 280
Round Pond, 284-285

Saline County Conservation Area, **22-
    25**
Saline County State Fish & Wildlife
    Area, 23-25
Saline Springs, **18-21**
Sammons Creek Trail, **264-267**

Section 8 Woods State Nature Preserve,
    122-125
Seed ticks, 7
Sentry Bluff Trail, 85
Shawnee National Forest, 2
Sierra Club, x
Signal Point Trail, 103
Slave House, 19
snakes, 9-10
Southern Illinois University, 167, 169,
    175
Southeast Missouri State University,
    282
spiders, 8-9
Stone Face, **26-27**
Stone Face Recreation Site, **26-28**

Table Rock, 41
Tatum Heights Park in Carbondale, 167
ticks, 7
topographical maps, 6
Touch of Nature Environmental Center,
    175-179
Tower Rock, **66-69**, 215, 216
Tower Rock Recreation Area, **66-69**
Trail of Tears, **238-243**
Trail of Tears State Forest, 241, 242
Trillium Trail, 182, 183
tupelo trees, 123
Turkey Bayou Recreation Areas, **208-
    213**
Twin Trees Park, 282

Union County Conservation Area, **252-
    255**

Walk-Away Trail, 187
Waterfall Trail at Ferne Clyffe, 151
White Pine Trail, **230-233**
White Trail, 85
Wickliffe Mound, 277
wilderness areas, 5
William Marberry Arboretum, 167, 168
Wildcat Bluff, **110-115**
Wildlife Nature Trail, 23, 25
Woodland Indians, 99, 149
Woodland World Trail, 175

ID